Access your Online Resources

"Help! What Do I Do Now?" is accompanied by a number of printable online materials, designed to ensure this resource best supports your professional needs

Go to https://resourcecentre.routledge.com/speechmark and click on the cover of this book

Answer the question prompt using your copy of the book to gain access to the online content.

"Help! What Do I Do Now?"

"Help! What Do I Do Now?" is an essential guide for primary school teachers, full of practical strategies to support children with social, emotional and mental health (SEMH) needs in the classroom.

The book offers a comprehensive approach and holistic perspective on SEMH support, covering topics from regulating the whole class and regulating individual children, to understanding the impact of sensory needs and transitions. Chapters illustrate how a range of strategies can be applied in real-life classrooms, and case studies and reflections demonstrate how they can be adapted to suit each setting and unique child in need. Further support and guidance is also offered on staff wellbeing, emphasising the importance of looking after yourself and supporting your own wellbeing first.

With a wealth of cost and time effective ideas and suggestions to support children with SEMH, this accessible guide will be essential reading for practising and trainee primary school teachers, as well as SENCOs and school leaders.

Sharon Cooke is a Thrive Licensed Practitioner and nurture specialist who has extensive experience of working in schools with vulnerable children with a wide range of additional needs including social, emotional, behavioural and SEND needs. She is also a member of the Brighter Futures Nurture Outreach Team providing training and coaching for school staff.

Sonia Mainstone-Cotton is a freelance nurture specialist and Thrive Licenced Practitioner working with Brighter Futures Nurture Outreach team, she has extensive experience of working in schools and early years settings with children who have high social, emotional and mental health needs. Sonia also delivers training across the country, working with early years settings, charities and schools. This is Sonia's 12th book.

"Help! What Do I Do Now?"

Strategies to Support Children with Social, Emotional and Mental Health Needs in the Primary Classroom

Sharon Cooke and
Sonia Mainstone-Cotton

Routledge
Taylor & Francis Group

LONDON AND NEW YORK

Designed cover image: Cover artwork created by Orla aged 5, Ramona aged 7, and Luca aged 9

First published 2025
by Routledge
4 Park Square, Milton Park, Abingdon, Oxon OX14 4RN

and by Routledge
605 Third Avenue, New York, NY 10158

Routledge is an imprint of the Taylor & Francis Group, an informa business

© 2025 Sharon Cooke and Sonia Mainstone-Cotton

The right of Sharon Cooke and Sonia Mainstone-Cotton to be identified as authors of this work has been asserted in accordance with sections 77 and 78 of the Copyright, Designs and Patents Act 1988.

All rights reserved. No part of this book may be reprinted or reproduced or utilised in any form or by any electronic, mechanical, or other means, now known or hereafter invented, including photocopying and recording, or in any information storage or retrieval system, without permission in writing from the publishers.

Trademark notice: Product or corporate names may be trademarks or registered trademarks, and are used only for identification and explanation without intent to infringe.

British Library Cataloguing-in-Publication Data
A catalogue record for this book is available from the British Library

Library of Congress Cataloging-in-Publication Data
Names: Cooke, Sharon author | Mainstone-Cotton, Sonia author
Title: Help! what do I do now? : strategies to support children with social, emotional and mental health needs in the primary classroom / Sharon Cooke and Sonia Mainstone-Cotton.
Description: Abingdon, Oxon : Routledge, 2025. | Includes bibliographical references and index. | Contents: Regulating a whole class — Regulating an Individual Child — The environment — Sensory — Transitions — Creativity — Staff wellbeing — Resources. | Identifiers: LCCN 2024049119 (print) | LCCN 2024049120 (ebook) | ISBN 9781032739786 hardback | ISBN 9781032739748 paperback | ISBN 9781003467021 ebook
Subjects: LCSH: Children with social disabilities—Education (Primary) | Children with mental disabilities—Education (Primary) | Primary school teaching | Classroom management | Children with mental disabilities—Behavior modification
Classification: LCC LC4065 .C665 2025 (print) | LCC LC4065 (ebook) | DDC 371.9—dc23/eng/20250131
LC record available at https://lccn.loc.gov/2024049119
LC ebook record available at https://lccn.loc.gov/2024049120

ISBN: 978-1-032-73978-6 (hbk)
ISBN: 978-1-032-73974-8 (pbk)
ISBN: 978-1-003-46702-1 (ebk)

DOI: 10.4324/9781003467021

Typeset in Optima
by codeMantra

*Sonia dedicates: thanks to The Brighter Futures team,
you are the best team to work with*

Sharon dedicates: thanks to Sonia – Thank you for your encouragement to break out and do something new, for including me in this project and pointing me in the right direction through the process. You are a great friend and colleague.

And to my lovely Mum – Thanks for everything

Contents

	Introduction	1
1	Regulating a Whole Class	19
2	Regulating an Individual Child	28
3	The Environment	40
4	Sensory Needs	53
5	Transitions	61
6	Creativity	80
7	Staff Wellbeing	97
8	Resources	117
	Conclusion	152
	Index	155

Introduction

Introduction

We hope this book will assist you with some ideas and resources for supporting children in your classroom who have social, emotional and mental health needs (SEMH). Sharon and I (Sonia) both work for a small organisation in Bath and North East Somerset called Brighter Futures. We are both peripatetic nurture workers supporting early years and primary-aged children in school who have been identified as having high SEMH needs. Our role is to help the child and the staff, offering ideas and suggestions, and being there for all involved. We are two members of a small multi-disciplinary team of 14, and in our team we have a range of experience from an infant school head teacher, educational psychologist, SENDCos, paediatric and adolescent psychotherapist, early years educator, forest school lead, art therapist, teaching assistants, occupational therapist and social worker. This book is going to share with you many of the ideas, strategies and tools we use in our role. We are hoping that you will find some ideas and tools that might help you.

Why we wrote this book

We have the privilege of working in many different schools across our local authority, every day we see different children, teachers, teaching assistants and senior leaders. Currently, between us we are working in

18 different schools. We know that every school is different, but we also know that since the pandemic in the UK, it feels harder in schools. The needs we are seeing in school are higher, we know that currently there is less funding in schools (although we are hopeful that will change), and we know that many teachers and senior leaders feel under a huge amount of pressure. We are not pretending that this book will fix all of that, but we have seen an increased need for staff to feel supported, aided and skilled, so we wanted to be able to offer a few ideas that might go some way to offering some support and skills.

What is SEMH?

Social, emotional and mental health (SEMH) is a phrase that we are hearing increasingly. SEMH needs are part of the SEND (special educational needs and disability) Code of Practice and have been so since 2015. The SEND Code of Practice describes SEMH needs thus:

> Children and young people may experience a wide range of social and emotional difficulties which manifest themselves in many ways. These may include becoming withdrawn or isolated, as well as displaying challenging, disruptive or disturbing behaviour. These behaviours may reflect underlying mental health difficulties such as anxiety or depression, self-harming, substance misuse, eating disorders or medically unexplained physical symptoms. Other children and young people may have disorders such as attention deficit disorder, attention deficit hyperactive disorder or attachment disorder.
> (UK Government, 2015, Paragraph 6.32)

In our team, we view SEMH within a model of difference rather than within a deficit model. We are all on an SEMH needs continuum, we all require to have our SEMH needs met. As educators, we need to support children's SEMH needs wherever we find them and this can be varied; SEMH needs can be shown through different ways. We believe that behaviour is one way in which a child communicates to us and sometimes it can be incredibly tricky to understand the nuance of what a child is trying to tell us.

> **MOMENT FOR REFLECTION**
>
> Just for a moment think about your own SEMH needs, how do you communicate these? I know for me (Sonia), when I am stressed, I can be quite snappy and intolerant to my direct family, without saying I am stressed, but my behaviour shows I am. For Sharon, her SEMH needs show in defensive responses to people. When I am stressed, I hear things through a self-critical filter and I begin to analyse conversations and can feel people are being negative about me. Generally, this is inaccurate.
>
> It's the same with the children we work with, sometimes they will show us through shouting or swearing at us, or they may hit out, kick, run away, hide or freeze or many other behaviours. Often not using the words alongside to identify what is specifically going on for them, this might be because they don't know and are unable to name it, but they feel it.

A friend of mine, Tamsin Grimmer, suggests we all need to learn to be behaviour detectives, using detective-type skills to discover what the child is trying to tell us (Grimmer, 2022). I find this phrase so helpful, I think it describes so well one of the skills we need as educators.

How do SEMH needs show themselves?

The way SEMH needs appear will vary hugely from person to person, but below are some ways you might see them manifest in the classroom:

- shouting out
- picking skin/pulling hair
- self-harming
- running off
- hiding
- being withdrawn
- struggling to make friends

- selective mutism
- hurting others
- struggling to concentrate
- often hungry
- often tired
- throwing objects at others/across spaces
- struggling to sit still
- agitated
- scared
- laughing inappropriately at people/incidents
- refusing to join in
- looking sad
- making themselves as small as they can (e.g., curling their body up)
- crying
- baby talk or silly voices

It is so easy to see some of these behaviours and presume that the child is intentionally trying to be difficult, they dislike us or they just don't care for learning. With the children we work with, the child is sometimes displaying some incredibly painful and challenging behaviours which is extremely hard for everyone involved, and this is often coming from a place of hurt, fear or feeling unsafe. Mona Delahooke's (2019) book has some excellent diagrams and insights which show us how children might be presenting and what might be going on in their heads and bodies. As a team, we have all used her book a lot. We recognise that as educators it can be incredibly hard to manage when a child is dysregulated and struggling, particularly when you are in a classroom and the child does not have additional support from another adult. That is the reason we are writing this book, to offer some glimmers of ideas that might support you.

What contributes to SEMH needs?

There can be many reasons why our SEMH needs can be triggered, sometimes this is linked to experiences or the environment, but not always. There are some areas which should alert us to the potential of a child having higher SEMH needs:

- a child who has experienced trauma
- a child who is looked after or adopted
- a child who has moved house
- a child who moved country
- a child who has a new sibling or becomes a blended family
- a break-up in the family
- a bereavement in the family
- close family member with mental health difficulties
- close family member with serious physical health difficulties
- being a young carer
- drug/alcohol abuse in the home
- foetal alcohol spectrum disorder
- domestic violence in the home
- stress in the home due to finance
- serious physical illness in the child
- post-traumatic stress disorder
- neurodiversity

However, it also needs to be pointed out that sometimes we don't know, it is not always obvious, and we are not always able to link it to something specific. In this book, we are not going to go into detail exploring these specific areas, but you can find recommendations of books and resources in the further reading section which do give information on these specific areas. Our book will offer strategies and ideas that support children who are struggling, for whatever reason.

Figures for SEMH

The figures released in 2023 from the UK government national statistics show that there were 1,183,384 children in England who were recognised as having SEN needs in education, this was up by 4.7 per cent from 2022 (UK Government, 2023). Of this number, 229,723 were recognised as having SEMH needs and 54,598 had an EHCP (education health care plan). For anyone working in schools, this won't come as a big surprise, as we have been saying it feels like the needs are increasing, and these statistics show us they are.

MOMENT FOR REFLECTION

Just for a moment think of the children you work with and which ones you think might be showing higher SEMH need. Now spend a moment to consider if you know what might be behind that. Also, think about those children who are not currently showing high needs, but knowing something about their story might indicate to you that they are more vulnerable.

Mental health in children and young people

In 2023, the NHS England produced a report suggesting one in 5 children and young people had a probable mental health difficulty (NHS England, 2023). This is based on the number of children and young people who have been referred to services, this was for children and young people aged 8–25. We know that COVID-19 had a big impact on the mental health of many people, including children and young people. In 2022, the BBC reported that there had been a 77 per cent rise in the number of children needing specialist support for severe mental health crises (BBC, 2022). I know many teachers and teaching assistants who feel they do not have the relevant training and education in supporting children's mental health. I sympathise with this feeling. I always encourage the staff I work with to read up about the area, become as informed as they can and attend any training they can. There are a rising number of courses available and also tools which can assist, such as Thrive (https://www.thriveapproach.com/), which is a tool used by most of the schools in our area and we use it in our team. Thrive describes itself as "a trauma-informed, whole school or setting approach to improving the mental health and wellbeing of children and young people". The Anna Freud charity website is also an excellent resource with many articles, training and resources all on wellbeing and mental health (https://www.annafreud.org/). At the end of this chapter, we have listed some useful further resources to support you in this subject.

Designated mental health lead

In the 2017 government Green Paper on transforming children and young people's mental health provision, they announced the plan to have a mental health lead in every school by 2025. Their role is to do the following:

- oversee the help the school gives to pupils with mental health problems
- help staff to spot pupils who show signs of mental health problems
- offer advice to staff about mental health
- refer children to specialist services if they need to do so

(UK Government, 2017)

Funding is currently available until 2025 for the leads to have the relevant training. It is usually a member of the SLT (senior leadership team), sometimes the SENDCo (special educational needs coordinator), who takes on this role. The purpose of this role is not to diagnose a mental health condition, but to lead the whole school's approach to mental health, to share an understanding with other staff and be able to know when and where to signpost to other agencies. Ideally, you should know who the mental health lead is in your school, if you don't know, do go and find out.

It is widely recognised that there needs to be a whole school approach to mental health and the designated mental health lead is one part of that. The National Institute for Health and Care Excellence (NICE, 2022) proposes that every education setting needs to adopt a whole-school approach to supporting the positive social and emotional wellbeing of all children and staff in their setting. They suggest that part of this is having a culture and ethos that promote relational approaches and inclusion and understand the importance of psychological safety. They also recommend that all settings have an understanding of trauma-informed approaches. All schools should have a wellbeing and/or mental health policy; these policies should be regularly updated and all staff should be aware of them. If you haven't read yours for a while, it might be worth looking at it and reminding yourself what is in it.

Mental health support team (MHST)

The NHS have a new service now working in schools called mental health support team (MHST). This service aims to support the mental health needs of children and young people in primary, secondary and further education. They aimed to have just under 400 MHSTs in schools by the end of 2023 and more than 500 by the Spring of 2024. It is worth looking in your area to see what is happening, as it is being delivered in slightly different ways across the country. In our area (Bath and North East Somerset), it is being delivered through Camhs (child and adolescent mental health services), they are offering 6–8 sessions of cognitive behavioural therapy (CBT) with secondary-aged pupils and to parents/carers of primary-aged children to support their child. They work with children who are experiencing low mood, low self-esteem and with behavioural difficulties. They target those children who have recognised mental health difficulties but are not at the higher level that we usually make a Camhs referral for. In our area, the referral is made by the designated mental health lead in the school directly to the MHST. This is something you may be familiar with already, but if not, find out if you have access to this service in your school.

How do we know if a child in your class is struggling with SEMH needs?

As mentioned above, there can be many different reasons why a child may have higher SEMH needs. We hope that as teachers you will have some key information about each child in your class, such as who they live with, whether they are a looked after child or adopted. Hopefully, you would also know key information, such as if a parent has died or the parents have recently separated or if there are concerns regarding domestic violence, drug and alcohol misuse in the home. However, we are aware that you are not always given this type of information. This type of information is useful as it will alert you to the possibility that the child may have higher SEMH needs, helping you to be more aware and vigilant and, hopefully, be able to give extra support if it is needed. If you have a child in your class who is a looked after child or a previously looked after child, there will be a lead teacher in the school with responsibility for looked after children. It is worth finding out who that lead teacher is and having a conversation with them about the needs of the child and how you can best support them.

Going back to Tamsin Grimmer's comment about being a behaviour detective, the main way we will know a child is struggling with SEMH needs is by being observant. Noticing and watching and being aware of differences. Every child is different and will show their needs in various ways, but as we get to know the children we work with and begin to learn about the way they communicate, how they are, and their preferences; we are then in a better position to begin to notice when their needs are higher. This is, of course, tricky at the start of the year with a new class or cohort of children, but hopefully, you will have been able to have a handover from their previous teacher or nursery (if they are in early years) to find out a few key things about the child. I would encourage you to ask questions to previous staff or the SENDCo and be curious, as well as find out what you can about the children. Also ask questions such as, are there any triggers for particular children that I need to know about? We will cover these further as we go through the book, as knowing what triggers/agitates/upsets a child can be extremely useful information and help you to plan more effectively.

Observations

My background (Sonia) is in early years, so observations are a key part of an early years toolkit, and this is a tool that we also use a lot in our team. When we first start working with a child, we always make several observations of the child, before we start any direct work. The observations allow us to watch and see what might be happening, the child's body language, what is going on around the child, as well as how they are behaving. I recognise that we are in a unique position in our role that we can stand back and observe, and this is not always possible for teachers, however, if you can find some time to do this, I would highly recommend it. If there is a moment in the class day when you have the class doing things that don't need your immediate attention, or if you can get another adult in the room to manage the class while you stand and observe for 20–30 minutes, this can be hugely beneficial. Also observing in different situations, for example, in the dinner hall, or in the playground. There are some useful tools which many schools use for monitoring a child's behaviour, especially when they are experiencing challenging behaviour. One of these is the A, B, C chart, which stands for:

A = Antecedent: what happened before the incident?
B = Behaviour: what was the behaviour?
C = Consequences: what was the consequence of this?

In our team, we have added an F to this:

F = Function: what is the function of the behaviour?

Sometimes these are used as a running record of what is happening in a day or week, and that is good, but it is especially helpful to be able to use it to understand what is going on, to discover if there are any particular triggers. These triggers might be specific other children, staff or activities, or transitions. Is the behaviour always the same or does it vary? The ABCF tool is useful as it can help us to think about what the function might be, for example, the child might be seeking connection with an adult, or they might be needing a sensory reduction so the consequence of being put outside of the classroom has met their need. This comes back to the behaviour being a communication, we need to understand what is being communicated to us and why.

CASE STUDY 0.1

One little boy Sonia worked with recently began to have some big moments of dysregulation throughout the day, there had been a significant change in the family situation, so the behaviour wasn't a big surprise. However, the school were struggling to see what the triggers might be. They used the ABCF tool over a few days to try and track what was happening to help them understand. Through using the tracker over a few days they realised there was a pattern with the times he became dysregulated and these were times when the class were in more of a self-choice mode and there were lots of children moving around. This little boy found it challenging when too many children were in a space and moving about. The staff team adjusted their plans, they created four groups and had a plan for two groups at a time to be inside and two groups outside during the self-choice time. This provided a structure which worked for several children, gave them more space for them to move about in and it lowered the stress levels for this particular boy which led to fewer moments of dysregulation.

Another useful observation tool is one used more commonly in early years, but I think it also has benefits across primary ages. It is called the Leuven scale. It was designed by Ferre Laevers and Leuven University, and it is a five-point scale which enables educators to measure a child's wellbeing and involvement. I find this an incredibly useful scale with children where we have concerns about their SEMH. When a child has a high level of involvement and high wellbeing, they will be involved in their learning, but when they are middling or low, their ability to learn is much lower. It is often obvious when a child is deeply involved in something but sometimes it is easier to miss some of the signs of the child who is middling and lower. This tool can help us to identify and understand when they are engaged and what it is that engages them. It is a tool to use several times to gain a deeper understanding of the child, helping you to get a clearer picture of what they engage in and what they don't engage in, helping you to see when they might appear to be doing the actions, and following the instructions but actually in practice they are reluctant, or have a low engagement. The Structural Learning website (https://www.structural-learning.com/post/leuven-scale-a-teachers-guide) has a useful article written for teachers about using this tool and the Leicestershire City Council website (https://resources.leicestershire.gov.uk/education-and-children/early-years/early-years-foundation-stage-eyfs/learning-development-and-assessment/wellbeing-and-involvement) has a link to the forms you can use.

Emotional literacy

One of the key areas we work on in our role is helping children (and staff sometimes) to have a broad range of emotional literacy. The more I do this work, the more I have realised that this is crucial. We all experience a complex range of emotions and feelings and it is so important we can understand what these are and to be able to name them and recognise what is going on in our bodies. Brene Brown has written a useful book called *Atlas of the Heart* (2021) and she explores and names 87 different emotions. She started writing this book after doing some research with over seven thousand students and found that the average number of emotions they could name and recognise were three: Happy, Angry and Sad. In her book, she suggests that "language is our portal to meaning-making, connection, healing, and learning", I find that phrase so helpful.

We need a wide range of words to understand what is happening to us, to be able to make sense of what is going on and, with this, we need to understand what our needs are. If it has got to mid-morning, and I missed breakfast, and if someone has asked me a question and I don't know the answer, I might be feeling flustered, I might be getting hot and agitated, I might snap at my friend. If my emotional vocabulary is limited, I might say I'm angry, but I am probably feeling hungry, a bit overwhelmed, maybe a bit ashamed and embarrassed as I didn't know the answer. If I can recognise all of that, I can ask for some food, get a drink, acknowledge I am unsure and ask for help, but all that means recognising what is going on in my body and it needs a wider range of emotional vocabulary than just anger. The word anger doesn't describe it or help me to meet my needs.

The writer and researcher who has changed a lot of thinking about how we teach emotions to children and how we understand emotions is Lisa Feldman Barrett (2018). She raises questions about our practice of using a limited number of images of faces in our teaching to children about emotions. This is a common resource that we have all used in our team and many schools use, I have many emotion tools with usually up to eight faces, and we often ask children to identify where they are on the emotion faces. Lisa Feldman Barrett's criticism of this is that it is coming from an assumption that there is an emotion centre and blueprint of emotions in our brain. Her research disputes this. One of the difficulties she has with using faces to link to emotions is that the same facial expression can be used to show many different emotions. For example, the face of someone screaming could be showing someone terrified that they have seen a mouse, or it could be someone who is screaming in pain because they have broken their leg, or it could be someone screaming in pleasure they have just won an unexpected award, or it could be someone screaming at the anticipation of seeing someone they adore. If we only see the face and not the surrounding context, we can't know what the emotion is. Also, emotions can show themselves in different ways, when I am feeling joyful, sometimes I smile, sometimes I laugh and at times I cry when I have felt a huge sense of joy. I cried when I saw my daughters after giving birth, that was a huge sense of joy and relief that they were safe and I burst into tears.

But what does this mean for our practice with children? I still use emotion tools but rather than asking children to identify with a particular face, I use them more to have wider conversations and I try to introduce as many different emotional words as I can into my work. This is sometimes through the use of stories and expanding on what might be going on in the story and also through the "I wonder" phrase. The "I wonder" phrase is one we use a lot in our team, rather than telling a child how they are feeling, we wonder about the situation. I might say, "Bas, I am wondering if you are feeling frustrated and disappointed because you want to go outside and play but I have said you need to finish your maths." By using the "I wonder" phrase. you are not telling a child how they feel, because none of us can know how another person feels, but you can offer some curiosity and help the child to think about what might be going on for them. My takeaway from Brene and Lisa's work is to become more emotionally literate and to teach a much wider emotional vocabulary and understanding to the children I work with.

MOMENT FOR REFLECTION

Just for a moment think about your emotional vocabulary and understanding, how emotionally literate are you? We can only share a rich emotional literacy with children if we have this ourselves. This might be an area you want to read more about. I would highly recommend Brene Brown's (2021) book for this, it is a book I regularly go back to.

Window of tolerance

This is an area that is crucial for our understanding of ourselves and the children we work with. This term was originally created by Dan Siegel (2020) to help us understand when we can cope. There will always be times in our lives when we can cope and this is known as our window of tolerance. When we are within our window of tolerance, we can manage our everyday challenges and everyday life events, we are also able to manage and process new information, decisions and instructions. When we are in our window of tolerance, there will be some variables and ups and downs, but we will be able to cope. When we move outside of our window of tolerance, we can find it difficult to manage and cope with everyday experiences and challenges, taking instructions can be a challenge and making decisions may be hard. Everyone has a window of tolerance but everyone's window of tolerance is a different size, for some, their window is much narrower, and sometimes our window also becomes narrower.

MOMENT FOR REFLECTION

Take a moment to think about when you have been outside your window of tolerance. Lack of sleep is a big problem for me that puts me outside my window. I find it hard to make decisions and I become very snappy due to lack of sleep.

We use this model a lot in our team to explain to staff, parents and older children as a way of understanding some feelings and behaviours. It is particularly useful for understanding when a child is unable to cope with the usual everyday small routines and transitions, this shows us that their window of tolerance that day is much narrower and we need to adapt to support them. Many things can impact our window of tolerance becoming smaller, for example, illness, poor diet, lack of sleep, life changes, and stress. But there are things we can do to help our window get bigger, minimising stress, experiencing joy, being with others that we love, supportive relationships, achieving or mastering something. These can all help to build resilience and increase our windows.

As adults working with children, our job is to help strengthen and widen each child's window of tolerance. There is a useful YouTube video from Hampshire Child and Adolescent Mental Health Service that explains the window of tolerance in more detail: www.youtube.com/watch?v=K1ovJu2GNVo

Every child is different

It is an obvious thing to say, but every child in your class is different, every child we work with has their special ways, interests and uniqueness; our job is to discover and learn about them. As the year progresses, you will learn about the uniqueness of each child, you will learn which tools work, and which ones don't, and you will learn the sensory needs of the children and their preferred way to learn. We will revisit this throughout the book.

The structure of the book

Before I finish the Introduction, I will give you an idea about the structure of the book. Sharon and I have written this book together, some chapters Sharon has led on and others I have led, but each chapter is a combination of both our thoughts and experiences. Throughout the book, we are using the word "educator" to include all adults who work alongside children in school, regardless of their level of qualification or experience. We are using the term "parents" to include not only parents but also any main carers of a child, for example, grandparents, foster carers, or step-parents. Any children are referred to using a pseudonym. We have also tried to consider the representation of backgrounds, cultural heritage, settings and gender to try and ensure this book shares the perspective of others.

At the end of each chapter we have listed the references cited in that chapter and we have also listed some further resources that might be useful linked to the topics discussed in that chapter. Also, Chapter 8 has handouts and resources we have created that you might want to use.

The subjects we cover in this book are:

Regulating a whole class   Chapter 1
Regulating an individual child   Chapter 2

"HELP! WHAT DO I DO NOW?"

The environment	Chapter 3
Sensory needs	Chapter 4
Transitions	Chapter 5
Creativity	Chapter 6
Staff wellbeing	Chapter 7
Resources	Chapter 8

This is a book you might want to dip in and out of or you may choose to read it all the way through, there is no right or wrong way, we just hope it will be useful.

 Further resources

Websites

https://assets.publishing.service.gov.uk/media/5a901d6ce527 4a5e67567fc1/The_designated_teacher_for_looked-after_and_ previously_looked-after_children.pdf
https://www.mentalhealth.org.uk/
https://mentallyhealthyschools.org.uk/
https://www.youngminds.org.uk/professional/schools/

Books for adults

Bomber, L. (2020) *Know Me to Teach Me*. Broadway: Worth Publishing.
Chatterjee, R. (2018) *The Stress Solution: The 4 Steps to Calmer, Happier, Healthier You*. London: Penguin.
Haines, S.(2016) *Trauma Is Really Strange*. London: Singing Dragon.
Johnson, S. (2024) *All About SEMH: A Practical Guide for Primary Teachers*. Abingdon: Routledge.

Mainstone-Cotton, S. (2021) *Supporting Children with Social, Emotional and Mental Health Needs in the Early Years*. Abingdon: Routledge.

Mosley, B. (2023) *Happy Families: How to Protect and Support Your Child's Mental Health*. London: Bluebird.

Smith, J. (2022) *Why Did Nobody Tell Me This Before?* London: Penguin.

Books for children

Dowrick, C. and Martin, S. (2015) *Can I Tell You About Depression?* London: Jessica Kingsley Publishers.

Eland, E. (2020) *When Sadness Comes to Call*. London: Anderson Press.

James, A. and Stowell, L. (2018) *Looking After Your Mental Health*. London: Usborne.

References

BBC (2022) Children mental health: Huge rise in severe cases, BBC analysis reveals. Available at: https://www.bbc.co.uk/news/education-60197150

Brown, B. (2021) *Atlas of the Heart*. London: Vermilion.

Delahooke, M. (2019) *Beyond Behaviours*. London: John Murray.

Feldman Barrett, L. (2018) *How Emotions Are Made*. London: Pan Macmillan.

Grimmer, T. (2022) *Supporting Behaviour and Emotions in the Early Years*. Abingdon: Routledge.

NHS England (2023) One in five children and young people had a probable mental disorder in 2023. Available at: https://www.england.nhs.uk/2023/11/one-in-five-children-and-young-people-had-a-probable-mental-disorder-in-2023/

NICE (National Institute for Health and Care Excellence) (2022) Social emotional and mental wellbeing in primary and secondary education. Available at: https://www.nice.org.uk/guidance/ng223/chapter/recommendations#whole-school-approach

Siegel, D. (2020) *The Developing Mind*. New York: Guildford Press.

UK Government (2015) SEND Code of Practice. Available at: https://assets.publishing.service.gov.uk/media/5a7dcb85ed915d2ac884d995/SEND_Code_of_Practice_January_2015.pdf

UK Government (2017) Green Paper on children and young people's mental health. Available at: https://www.gov.uk/government/consultations/transforming-children-and-young-peoples-mental-health-provision-a-green-paper/quick-read-transforming-children-and-young-peoples-mental-health-provision

UK Government (2023) Gov.uk statistics: special educational needs in England. Available at: https://explore-education-statistics.service.gov.uk/find-statistics/special-educational-needs-in-england

1 | Regulating a Whole Class

Introduction

We have all stepped into a room and sensed that the atmosphere is off. Something is not right or we feel anxiety moving about the environment. We look around and try to allay our misgivings by checking that we and others in the room are safe. Our senses search our memory to see if we have any recollection of previously coming through something similar successfully. We may even step physically closer to a friend or partner to give us the confidence to face whatever is coming. We will potentially breathe a little deeper or tense and relax our muscles to calm ourselves. However, what do we do if we are the only adult in the room in charge of 30 children, one of whom is dysregulated and is seriously having an impact on the other children in the classroom?

It is very easy for that one dysregulated child to tip other children into the same state as themselves. They might be showing their dysregulation by moving quickly and unsafely around the room, shouting, even crying, perhaps throwing things and becoming very distressed. This will make the other children feel vulnerable and scared and may cause further distress in the classroom. After all, emotions are catching, and we can all get pulled into an anxiety dance, feeding one another's feelings and adding fuel to the fire.

I (Sharon) would suggest that once a child, or a handful of children, have reached this level of dysregulation it would be difficult for one adult to give them the attention they need while also being in charge of the rest of the class. Therefore, it is helpful to have a few ideas and strategies to hand to nip things in the bud, stopping the escalation and the spread of unwanted behaviours.

Sonia and I have experienced this kind of setting over years of working in schools. It may be helpful for us to share some of the things we have found to be useful in calming whole classes and keeping everyone on an even keel.

As part of our work in schools, we always schedule observation sessions in the classroom when we carefully watch the children. During my observations, I look for the following signs:

- any fidgeting
- repeated movements
- putting fingers or other items in their mouth
- rubbing body or body parts on the floor or on the furniture
- pulling or hurting themselves (biting, pulling eyelids, etc.)
- tapping fingers or items in hands, usually a pen or pencil
- swinging often on a chair
- what the other children are doing. Is this child standing out as doing something different to the others around them?
- calling out
- disrupting others, including the adults
- how they follow whole class instructions
- does the child try to pull in another child or children into their behaviour? Notice how they seek attention.
- any unusual facial expressions/grimacing
- any unusual hand movements (flapping or posturing, etc.)

Any of these behaviours may suggest unrest and a build-up of emotional energy.

My top tip to any educator would be to try and take 30 minutes of your planning time once or twice a term to observe your class while someone else is in charge. At the beginning of the year, this is important as you get to know a new group. Having the luxury of standing back and simply watching will provide you with valuable information about the children in your care. It may offer valuable insight into how they behave before they erupt. By observing the children, you may spot signs of distress which can be your signal to interrupt the process of dysregulation before it gets to a high level.

CASE STUDY 1.1

I once worked with a child in Year one who regularly became violent. She would shout, hit anyone in her way, throw things and spit at people. After several incidents, I began to trace back in my mind what had happened just before the incident occurred. What was the trigger and what was the indication she was going to become unsettled? If her needs went unmet at this stage, she soon became dysregulated, affecting other children and often the whole class had to be evacuated from the classroom. I noticed that this girl always went slightly red in the face and pushed her right foot into the floor while raising and lowering her heel. I would not have noticed these small things if I had not taken the time to step back and watch her. These signs of agitation became my signal to act, distract, encourage a movement break or rub her back reassuringly. These things helped her to calm and remain in the classroom with her classmates for longer periods. The positive impact of interrupting her spin into dysregulation was that fewer people got hurt or spat at and so the other children were much keener to build a friendship with her. In time, this helped her feel understood, supported and liked by her peers. In fact, by Year 3 she was voted class representative on the school council.

MOMENT FOR REFLECTION

- What am I seeing?
- How often is the child engaging in a sensory-seeking behaviour? Mouthing, swinging, tapping, rubbing, pushing or pulling parts of the body?

Over the years it has been important for Sonia and me to know the particular needs of the children we work with. To help them, I try to match the need they are displaying with an appropriate solution.

- If I see a child putting lots of things in their mouth, I would suggest giving them a chew toy.
- If the child is moving and fidgeting a lot, they may benefit from five-minute movement breaks throughout the day.
- If they are pushing their legs hard into the desk, perhaps a wobble board or a resistance strap on their chair legs would provide the sensory feedback they are looking for very simply, without having to leave their desk.
- If the child is finding it difficult to be still and there are big body movements, encouraging them to perform tensing and relaxing exercises can help them release the tension they are holding in their body so they can focus and be still for a bit longer.

Knowing your children is key. Understanding their responses, and noting the way they move and interact with one another so that you can spot the beginnings of unsettling and interrupt that anxiety dance rather than joining the dance and becoming part of keeping the music playing! The children will be looking to you to set the emotional tone for the whole class. If you become triggered and anxious yourself, this will feed the emotions in the room and heighten the children's dysregulation. It is important to understand yourself, know your own triggers and understand what helps you to calm yourself quickly and effectively. It is important to read Chapter 7 on Staff Wellbeing, where you are actively encouraged to think about ways of looking after yourself in order to be that emotionally strong and healthy adult in charge whom the children can trust, connect with and learn from.

It is always good practice to model to the children that you need to calm yourself and regulate too. Brene Brown, an American professor, social worker and author, explores this in her (2015) book, *Daring Greatly*. She talks about leaders being courageous enough to be vulnerable, without making it about winning or losing. Instead of vulnerability showing our weakness, it's the greatest measure of courage we can show people. Sometimes it is helpful to be willing to show a little vulnerability to help the children in our class understand emotions and how we can choose to respond to them. This lends itself perfectly to modelling and leading whole class regulation activities.

MOMENT FOR REFLECTION

What makes you feel anxious in the classroom?

- Is there a particular behaviour which always gives you an emotional response?
- What helps you to calm quickly?
- Is there something you could keep on your desk to help you to calm, e.g., hand cream for a hand massage, an essential oil roller or diffuser with a lovely calming smell, cold water to drink, an elastic band or fiddle toy on your wrist or in your drawer?
- Are you hungry/tired/thirsty?
- How can you share this vulnerability while modelling how to respond in a healthy way to the emotion you are experiencing?

It is important to look after your own needs first. You cannot support others successfully if you are not in a good place yourself.

Hot spots and suggested solutions

There are times during the day which will contribute to the unsettling of certain children in your class. These are mainly around transition points in the day when children stop one thing and move into another. They can be busy bustling times when children can feel overwhelmed. There can also be points in the day when the rules change and children find this difficult to manage and understand. Arriving at school and separating from a parent can be a difficult time for some. Coming back into class after playtimes can also be a tricky transition as well as the lead-in to going home. At these points, it is helpful to plan a few minutes around a regulating activity together, giving the children the message, "'I am here, you are safe, it's OK, I will be here tomorrow."

I have seen this put into practice well in some of the schools I work in.

The Start of the day

One school introduced a "First Fifteen Thrive time" across the whole school. Each class spend the first 15 minutes of the day engaging in an emotionally right time development activity which is nurturing and allows them to connect with their adults and peers in a fun way. Often this will be a game where rules need to be negotiated like a card game. This has helped support children who find that first transition into school in the morning much easier and the adults can be on hand to check in and support them if they are wobbly. The adult can then introduce them into a group and support the play if necessary. This is a positive and calm segway into the start of the day and the children are keen not to miss the fun so they want to arrive on time and get into school to join in.

Playtime

Most schools still ask children to line up in the playground before coming into the school after break times. This is often a time when there is noise, hustle and bustle which can heighten the whole class. I have watched a Year two class line up on the far side of a playground on which a sensory circuit had been painted. The teacher could see that quite a few of the class were not ready to head inside calmly. Instead, she led them back into school through the sensory circuit. She demonstrated to the children what to do and got herself and her class ready for learning in the process!

Lining up

Another Reception teacher played a quick game of "Simon says" while in the line. She used different tones to her voice, sped up and slowed down and got the children to breathe deeply as part of the game. It only needs to last a few minutes but can save a lot of time in the long run if it prevents an incident when you arrive in the classroom.

Tapping

One of my favourite experiences was seeing a child wandering around the playground tapping his fingers. I recognised this as part of the Tension Tapping Technique (TTT). Every class in the school spent time after playtimes tension tapping together. A simple cartoon was played for a few minutes and children and adults were encouraged to join in and copy the tension tapping routine. In this particular school, it had become accepted that tension tapping helped people calm quickly. It was perfectly acceptable and normal for a child who was struggling individually to draw on tools they had practised as a whole class in times of stress. It was also accepted by the other children as being a sign to give that child space to calm and regulate themselves. In Chapter 8 is some guidance for tapping.

There are lots of whole class activities online which you can access easily:

- Mindfulness activities
- Peer massage
- Playdough gym
- Tension Tapping
- Go noodle exercises
- Relax kids
- Simple classroom games like "Thumbs up, heads down" or "Simon says"

However, remember, to match the need with the correct kind of response:

- Do the class need fizzing up or calming down?
- Can they interact with their peers, or do they need to do the same activity individually alongside their peers?
- Are their bodies busy and their mouths loud?

Start by matching the mood and gradually bring the children down by slowing down, quietening down and demonstrating calmness yourself.

Investment pays dividends

Look at these interventions as an investment. You might spend a few minutes off curriculum if you engage in them properly, however, you might save yourself an hour of having to evacuate a whole class and potentially a long time trying to regulate an individual child in your care. The result of taking the time to invest in regulating your whole class at these HOT SPOT times will pay off. The children in your class will be far more likely to use the regulation techniques they have practised with the rest of their class when they are struggling individually. Children will grow their ability to empathise with others when they see them using the calming techniques they have learned together.

Conclusion

Managing a whole class singlehandedly is a skill. Seeing it done well is a joy, but we must acknowledge that budget cuts and reduced numbers of adults in school make this more difficult. However, it does not have to be an unachievable goal when we understand ourselves and the children in our care. I hope this chapter has made you consider what helps you to calm and how you can safely share your vulnerabilities with your class in order to train them to handle their emotions well. Hopefully, the points we have considered in this chapter will give you scope to think about things slightly differently and invest a little time in regulating yourself and your class to aid everyone's wellbeing.

 Resources

Further reading

Horwood, J. (2009) *Sensory Circuits: A Sensory Motor Skills Programme for Children*. Hyde, Cheshire: LDA.
Johnson, S. (2023) *All about SEMH: A Practical Guide for Primary Teachers*. Abingdon: Routledge.

Reference

Brown., B. (2015) *Daring Greatly*. London: Penguin.

2 | Regulating an Individual Child

In Chapter 1 we were thinking about how to regulate the whole class, and we offered ideas and suggestions that can support this. This chapter is going to look at some ways we can support an individual child in the class. We know that sometimes one child becoming dysregulated and not managing can take up so much time and attention and can have a knock-on effect with other children in the class. This chapter offers a few ideas on how we can identify what is happening and support that child.

There are many overlaps in this chapter with Chapter 4 which focuses on sensory needs, but in this chapter, we are going to think about why the child may be struggling and how we can notice and feel confident about how to intervene.

 MOMENT FOR REFLECTION

For a moment. reflect on how you can feel different on different days. You can wake up feeling grumpy or positive, rested or exhausted, carefree or as if you are carrying the world's burdens! How does this affect the way you interact with others around you? How do these feelings and the emotions they carry affect your ability to be patient, kind, thoughtful and empathetic to

DOI: 10.4324/9781003467021-3

others? How do these emotions affect your face? How do others see you?

It is worth considering how the way you go into your day may have a direct impact on the behaviour you see in your classroom that day.

Here are some simple things to consider which may help you get ready for a better day:

- Are you feeling rested or exhausted? Do you need to get to bed earlier?
- Are you worried about a particular problem which is stopping you resting? Is there someone you feel you could chat with to help solve the issue or offer you some practical or emotional support?
- Have you given yourself a peaceful moment before starting your day? Breathing/mindfulness gratitude practice/faith-based meditation.
- Have you refueled your brain and body with healthy food and drink?
- Have you exercised or spent some time outside recently?
- Have you prepared for the day ahead?
- Have you connected with a loved one and do you feel valued and loved?

These ideas are explored in more detail in Chapter 7, "Staff Wellbeing". I would encourage you to read it carefully and perhaps think about making some changes, if necessary, to give yourself the best opportunity to start the day well. Of course, we all have days when we feel under par or have received difficult news about a loved one and find it more difficult to be positive. Speaking personally, I can honestly say that putting wellbeing routines in place to support myself helps me cope better on the tough days. Without those regular things drip-feeding me, I would not have the resilience or tools to help myself regulate.

It is also worth acknowledging that the children we work with are no different to us in this respect. Different things will affect the way they act and react to others and various situations throughout the day. Keeping this in mind will help you deal with situations compassionately with care and consideration.

The start of the day

For some children, arriving at school is a challenge, they may have had a fight with their family on their journey in, they may not have had breakfast, they may not have slept well, and they might be feeling anxious about something in the day. In the Introduction, we wrote about the window of tolerance, for some children, when they arrive you can see immediately from the way they look and hold themselves that their window of tolerance is small.

How do we know a child is struggling at the start of the day?

- They have a tense body.
- They may have slumped shoulders.
- They may be frowning.
- They may be looking sad or be crying.
- They may appear completely shut down, and quiet and may not be interacting with anyone around them.
- They may take a long time to settle, finding all sorts of things to prevent them from sitting down and starting the day.
- They may seek out the adults and stay physically close to them.
- They may refuse to take their coat off or take their hood down.
- They may hide under a table or in a small corner, making themselves small.
- They may be very loud and busy in their body.

Any of these signs might be an indicator to us that the child may need some additional support at the start of the day to give them a boost.

How can we support the child at start of the day?

Do they need breakfast? Many of the schools we work with have a box of cereal or some fruit that they can offer to children during the day. One school provides breakfast bagels to all children every day so a child doesn't need to ask for breakfast. Children can help themselves to as much or as little as they want or need. This has removed the embarrassment of food poverty and has been a very helpful addition to the start of the school day routine.

Do they need to do a quiet calming activity? These might be:

- drawing
- colouring-in
- a jigsaw
- some Lego
- a fine motor skills activity like threading, lacing or painting with cotton buds
- sensory rice treasure hunt, where a few small beads are hidden before the start of school. The box is left on the table ready for the child to go to an agreed location and start on arrival.
- sorting activities – sorting playing cards into suits, pencils into colour pots
- sharpening pencils in a quiet corner
- a word search
- quiet reading in a reading corner in comfy cushions
- brushing hair or using a head or foot massager
- using hand cream for a hand massage
- playdough

Do they need a movement break before they join the class? You could use:

- rolling over a gym ball
- doing a hopscotch
- running between two fixed points on the playground
- press-ups or press against the wall
- chair press-ups, tensing and relaxing exercises
- following a sensory circuit
- climbing on play equipment in the playground
- swinging on a swing or hammock
- pulling on climbing bars
- pushing tyres around the playground
- jumping on a trampoline
- dancing to music

- squats
- star jumps
- bunny hops
- roly-poly
- crawling
- crab walking

Encourage the child to spend some time breathing deeply before transitioning back into the classroom.

Sensory circuits are especially good because they lead the child through a process of releasing pent-up tension and excess energy they may be holding in their body and help them relax, regulate and calm before heading back to class. We have seen Reception children getting to a point where they can use a sensory circuit independently and have even noticed when other children are becoming dysregulated and have suggested to them they might find it helpful to complete the circuit themselves!

Sensory circuits can be purchased online or made very simply by placing hand and foot shapes, taped lines, and finger gyms on walls and floors in corridors. This may be something your school considers investing in and installing in a corridor for any child to access. I have seen such a circuit in use in one of the schools I work in. Any child from Reception to Year 6 can have access to it when permitted by their teacher. The expectation is very clearly communicated that once the circuit is completed the child returns to class. The sensory circuit in this particular school is near to the SENDCo's office so she can keep an ear open for any strays and remind them where they need to be if necessary. It has been very useful and has been accessed by most of the staff in the school as a regulation tool.

CASE STUDY 2.1

Sharon worked with a child who found it very difficult to sit still. He struggled to communicate and the frustration of this led to lots of angry outbursts where people got hurt. In his class, there was a period where the children were expected to sit for the register and lunch register and then go straight into a phonics lesson. This was just too long for many of the children to sit still, particularly for this lad. He would roll on the carpet, hit and kick others around him and would become very loud and disruptive. I suggested that he needed a carpet tile to mark his territory when sitting on the carpet. Before coming to the carpet, I suggested he needed to complete a sensory circuit. This was to take place and be timetabled before coming to the carpet and following the registers before starting phonics. The change in his attention and ability to focus was incredible. He was able to sit, listen, understand and engage in the lesson alongside his peers. It was so successful that his teacher began to encourage him to complete the circuit before every carpet time learning session. He quickly became aware of when he needed to move and would put his hand up and ask for permission to complete his circuit if necessary. He never took advantage of this arrangement and only used it when he needed to. His teacher was flexible and understanding in accommodating his needs as she could see the benefits to his learning. This child made great progress socially and emotionally. His communication skills increased; and his confidence grew. As a result, his academic achievements increased and his willingness to participate in class learning dramatically increased.

Key transitions

For some children there are key transition times in the day that act as a trigger, this could be at the change of lesson, moving into break time or lunchtime, or changing for PE. In Chapter 5 we explore transitions in much more detail, including looking at micro transitions such as ending for lunch, but here are a few ways to support micro transitions.

How do we know a child is struggling with a micro transition?

- Younger children may start to flit around the classroom, having a go at everything that is on offer before the session ends.
- They may start to call out or make noises.
- They may become agitated in the run-up to the transition.

- They may start fidgeting or tapping objects.
- They may throw things or become aggressive towards others as the classroom becomes busy.
- They may hide.
- They may start rocking on their chair.
- They may ask to go to the toilet to avoid the change.
- They may wander around or even leave the classroom.
- They may seek out an adult and stay physically close to them.
- They may carry on with what they are doing and refuse to stop until they are ready.
- They may run away and feel they need to escape the situation.

How can we support the child in this change?

- Pre-warn of the change, let the individual child know a change is happening.
- Some children find a visual timetable useful or a now and next board.
- Some children find a timer helps them get ready for a change.
- If it is tidy-up time, assign a specific tidy-up role for the child in a quieter area of the classroom. They can still be involved in the process but may cope better.
- Verbally check in with the child during this time to see if they are OK and encourage them to keep going.
- Move physically closer to the child and lend your calm to them, helping them to ground and feel safe.
- Consider if the child needs a job to do while transitions are happening away from the rest of the class (see Case Study 2.2).

CASE STUDY 2.2

Sonia worked with a little boy this year who found the transition into lunch tricky, lunch time preparation in a Reception class can take a long time!, especially at the start of the school year. When the class were told it was time to get ready for lunch, he presumed that meant he could go into the lunch hall immediately. He wasn't able to cope with the

30 minutes of tidying up, washing hands, and lining up. The change the staff put in for him was to give him a job to do at this time. He would go to the toilet, wash his hands and then wash up the cups from the morning snack. This gave him something to do, he loved being in water and he liked having the responsibility of a job. Doing this job meant he did not have to wait for everyone else or be in the toilet area with groups of others. Before they put this small change in place, he was regularly getting into trouble by hurting other children and running around.

Certain subjects

For some children, some subjects can cause distress, this may be due to the child feeling they can't do it, they are fearful about getting something wrong and would rather not try than be seen to mess up. They may simply dislike the subject or not see the need for it. A child Sharon worked with could not understand the need for silent reading. She hated it and refused to join in. We chatted together about how being able to read opened up all sorts of opportunities, kept us safe if it was a danger sign or helped us be successful if we were following a recipe, for example. When she could appreciate the need and benefits of reading, she was much happier to engage in silent reading. She still admitted it was the worst part of her day but was able to join in with the rest of the class. These feelings can trigger children to become dysregulated.

How do we know a child is struggling with a certain subject?

- They may become disruptive, annoying other children, calling out.
- They may start singing or humming or drumming their fingers.
- They may refuse to join in.
- They may look for ways to prolong the starting point – looking for a pencil, sharpening a pencil, looking for a rubber in case they make a mistake, or talking to other children. Collecting more equipment than necessary just to delay the start of work.

- They may ruin their work.
- They may leave the classroom.

How can we support the child who is struggling with a certain subject?

- Chat with them and explain why what they are learning will benefit them in the long term. Can they understand the benefits to them personally?
- Consider if they need their own space to work. This might be their own desk or workstation.
- Do they need to be paired with another child who brings out the best in them?
- Do they have all their equipment on their desk ready to start, so there is no need to wander around delaying the start of work?
- Do they need the work to be chunked into sizeable pieces in order to feel they have any chance of completing it?
- Do they need you to set them a challenge of completing three questions before checking in with them again?
- Do you need to check in and be with them so they have the confidence to make a start?
- Would they find visual instructions on their desk easier to follow to remind them of what to do next?
- Would they respond to some reward system for completing a certain task in the day?
- Would they respond better to an in-tray with work in it that they have to complete before lunchtime? They can choose when they complete each sheet rather than having the pressure of producing the work within a given hour of the day.

The end of the day

Some children find leaving school a hard transition, this can be for a lot of different reasons, sometimes this is from anxiety about what they will encounter at home, and at other times it can be linked to the dislike of any bigger transition.

How do we know if a child is struggling at the end of the day?

- They may start to find lots of jobs to do or need to do just a bit more of…
- They may start to withdraw from the rest of the class/teacher.
- They may start to call out or annoy other children.
- They may start humming or drumming their fingers.
- They may cry.
- They may complain of feeling unwell.
- They may become loud and busy in their body.
- They may go into a freeze response.
- They may hide.
- They may run away.

How can we support a child at the end of the day?

The child may need to do a sensory calming activity at the end of the day. Many are listed in Chapter 4 and the resources in Chapter 8.

They may need to end the day in another part of the school. Some children we have worked with spend time with the SENDCo or a member of the senior leadership team at the end of the day. Not as a punishment but as a way to calmly end the day. One child Sonia worked with did this each day with the deputy head and they talked about sport for 10 minutes before it was time to go home. A child Sharon worked with exited the building via a different door, so it was less crowded and there wasn't an audience of parents watching his struggle as he left the classroom. Other children like to be at the front or the back of the line so they know exactly when they will leave and who will leave before and after them. One child Sharon worked with needed a snack before leaving school. This literally gave him the energy to face what was to come.

One major problem that we both have had to address in many schools is the fear of the child approaching the end of the day, knowing that a bad report will be delivered to a parent or that a parent will assume a bad report. In several situations, we have introduced a communication book. Any tricky issues can be written in the book, either from home or from school. This limits the need to pass on negative information in front of the child. Only positive comments can be delivered within the child's hearing. If the only positive thing which can be said at drop-off is "She put her shoes on herself this morning", then that is the only message passed on verbally. If the only positive message at the end of the day is, "He played with the Lego well today", then that is the message delivered. Children live up to what we say about them. I have often seen a child's confidence grow when they hear positive comments. Most children begin to want to live up to those comments and expectations and alter their behaviour accordingly. It is important to mention that this can often be more about managing the parent than the child. It can be difficult to manage but is necessary for the good and wellbeing of the child and maintaining your trusted relationship with them.

One of the schools Sharon works in makes a point of bookending the day with a regulating activity. It is a way of saying to the children, "I am here, you are safe, and I will be here tomorrow." It allows the relationship to be established at the start of the day and marks the point when the teacher hands the child over to another adult's care at the end of the day. It gives space and time for the child to focus on calming and relaxing, knowing the day is ending rather than frantically collecting belongings and dashing out of the building in a hurried and dysregulated state.

Relationship-building is crucial to supporting individuals in your class who struggle. They need to have their basic needs met and feel safe and special to someone. By building up a connected trusting relationship, you will be providing these things for the children in your care. You will get to know and understand them better, will spot their triggers more easily and therefore be able to step in to provide support in a timely manner rather

MOMENT FOR REFLECTION

Consider how you can stay connected to individuals in your class without being glued to them.

- Do you share interests with any of the children who struggle?
- Could you set aside any time each week, perhaps during assembly, when you could spend some one-to-one time playing a game, laughing together, getting to know and understand that child better?

than managing any fallout. You will become their co-regulator, teaching them how to calm themselves in time. As your relationship develops, and the trust deepens, the child will trust that you know what will help them and will be more open to accepting your suggestions. Often the teachers who take the time to invest in relationship-building are the teachers the children remember with fondness all their lives. What a privilege it is to have the opportunity to journey with a child in this way and watch them grow and flourish under our nurturing care.

Conclusion

In this chapter, we have thought about the importance of building a connected relationship with the child and becoming their co-regulator with a view to helping them develop the capacity to regulate themselves. When a child makes us feel frustrated and irritated sometimes, it can be very hard to want to spend time with them to get to know them well. It wouldn't necessarily be the first thing we would choose to do. However, learning to read the communications they are sending you through their behaviour will be key to helping you know how and when to intervene. I hope the ideas and suggestions shared in this chapter give you the confidence to try them out. I also hope you quickly see the benefits of investing in them.

 Resources

Further reading

Bomber, L. (2007) *Inside I'm Hurting*. Broadway: Worth Publishing.
Naish, S., Oakley, A., O'Brien, H., Penna, S., and Thrower, D. (2023) *The A–Z of Trauma-Informed Teaching Strategies and Solutions to Help with Behaviour and Support for Children Aged 3–11*. London: Jessica Kingsley Publishers.

3 | The Environment

In this chapter we will be exploring how the environment can impact a child, how it can affect their regulation, their behaviour, their mood – and yours – as well. In this chapter, we will be thinking about a range of environments around the classroom, the outdoors and other spaces around the school. We will be sharing examples from schools of how they have adjusted environments to support their children.

The physical environment that we spend time in can have a massive impact on us, it can affect our mood, and our ability to concentrate. There are environments where we walk in and feel a sense of this feels OK, it feels safe and calm, inviting, and I belong here. There are other environments where we step in and feel uneasy, on alert of what might happen, we might feel that we don't belong. Many different things can impact our sense of the environment, it could be the acoustics, the light levels, the number of items in the room, or the smell. We are going to explore ideas of how these can impact us and give some thought to how we can make tweaks to this. In Kerry Murphy and Fifi Benham's (2023) book, they have a section entitled "Mood zones", and they suggest it is useful for our spaces to have a space to relax, a space to react. This means a space where children regulate their emotions, a space to retreat, and for our rooms to be a space for us to regulate, where the space offers the opportunity to spend quality time with children.

THE ENVIRONMENT

 MOMENT FOR REFLECTION

Before we begin this chapter, if you can take a moment to look around your classroom, or if you are at home reading this, try and picture in your mind what your classroom looks like. Are there any parts of your classroom that you like? Are there any parts you would like to change? How do you think the children respond to your classroom? How does the classroom make you feel?

The third teacher

Reggio Emilia is a town in northern Italy, and it is famous in early years practice for its unique way of delivering early years education. Colleagues who work in the early years will probably be familiar with the name Reggio Emilia, but it's not so well known in other parts of primary education. Their unique way of education is by having a particular emphasis on creativity and the child's voice. The person credited with the approach of education in Reggio Emilia was a man called Loris Malaguzzi, who believed there are three teachers for children: adults, other children and the environment. He believed that the environment should be a place that is welcoming, aesthetically pleasing, a place that represents the cultures of your community and encourages exploration and learning. Although this is seen as an early years practice, I think there are aspects of this which can be adapted in other parts of primary education. If you take a look at Reggio Emilia classrooms (there is a link in the Resources section at the end of the chapter), you will see they create spaces which look inviting, with resources for children to use which promote enquiry and creativity. It is not unusual to see examples of nature inside the classroom; this is a small example but it can make a small aesthetically pleasing difference to the feel of a space. I also think the idea of how we make a space welcoming and one that represents the culture of our community is a good question to consider.

Making a welcoming space

We both work in a lot of different schools and classrooms and without a doubt, some spaces feel welcoming and others don't. Below are a few thoughts about how to help a space feel welcoming:

- have the photograph and name of staff on the door
- an uncluttered space
- using natural resources
- a visual timetable
- names or images on the wall of the children who belong in that class
- plants and flowers in the classroom
- a comfortable book corner with cushions or soft blankets
- an area that children can sit under or inside (canopy or tent)
- individual class name with a picture on the door
- information in the room about how this class fits in with the rest of the school
- a clean, comfy, brightly covered teacher chair with cushions
- a basket full of regulation toys for the whole class to access
- a regulation zone for a child to calm with appropriate books, toys, and sensory play items that are accessible to all
- a feelings check-in station, i.e., a space in the classroom which has visual reminders about feelings

Making a space that represents the culture of our community

It is so important that everyone in our community feels they are represented, and that they see examples of people like them and their community in the space. There are different ways we can do that in school, through the mix of images we use and the languages we have around, the range of books we have available representing all children. Having welcome signs in different languages is a good start, but that alone is not enough. Also celebrating Black History month is a good start but again it is not enough. A good starting point is to ask the people in your community about their cultural heritage and find out how you could represent that in your school and classroom. Dr Sharon Colilles is helpful in this area. In an interview she did for TTS, she discusses how we can make our work inclusive (TTS, n.d.). One question she asks is, can the children see themselves in the curriculum and our spaces? She reminds us that culture is not fixed, it is fluid and it changes rapidly as society changes. How are we reflecting that in our educational settings? She encourages us to know the children we work with and understand their cultural and ethnic identities of the children we work with, she encourages us to ask about the different cultural identities that the children bring with them, to be curious and enquire about these and to ask about the multiple languages that might be used in the home context.

Why does the physical environment make a difference?

For some of the children we work with, particularly those with high SEMH needs or/and neurodiversity needs, the classroom environment can be a hugely challenging space. There can be many different reasons for this, and some of these it is hard for us to change, but there can be some adaptations we can make. Below we are going to look at a few areas that can be tricky for some children.

Space to move

Is there room to easily move around your classroom? Each classroom will be different, particularly for different ages, in the early years there will be fewer desks and chairs and more space for play, but as we go up the years, this changes. But the layout of the room, having a sense of being able to move around, can be important. Also thinking about where we put children in the classroom. Many classes from Year one upwards will have a physical space for each child, their own spot in the classroom, in the younger years this is often a carpet spot. Often our natural inclination is to put the children we have most concern about at the front, nearest to us, but this isn't always the best option. Some children prefer sitting at the back, as this feels less threatening. Your inclination may be that if they are at the back, you are less likely to see what they are doing, but for the child, if they are at the back, they can see everything that is going on. Many children who have high SEMH needs often feel a strong sense of threat and danger, they are often hyper-vigilant, but if they are sitting at the back of the classroom, they don't need to worry about what is happening behind them. Some children with sensory processing needs find it easier to sit on the floor if their back is pushed against a table leg or a wall. Other children need a carpet tile which is exclusively for their use. This marks their area and ensures no other child invades their personal space.

CASE STUDY 3.1

Sonia had one little boy who had extremely high SEMH needs. When he moved into his new classroom the teacher put him near the front of the class, near her, as she knew that her connection with him was important, and she wanted him to feel she was near him, for reassurance. However, she quickly found he was constantly looking around him, getting up, walking around the classroom. After a few days she spoke to him about this and he told her he needed to see things. She asked if moving him to the back of the classroom would be better and he said yes, he would be able to see everything. Of course, this didn't fix everything but it did offer some reassurance to him and minimised how much he moved around.

A sense of my space

An important part of feeling a sense of belonging, that we all need, is having a feeling of my space. If children have their own desk space or carpet space, they will often have a strong sense of injustice if that spot is taken by someone else. If you are working with older children and they have a desk space, do you enable them to make it their own? This might be by getting them to design their name labels which you laminate and each child has

THE ENVIRONMENT

one of these on the desk, or they might be allowed their pencil case. Small things like this can make a difference to a feeling of belonging. If they have their own carpet space, make sure other children don't take this space, remind them all they each have their own space and need to keep to this.

MOMENT FOR REFLECTION

Just for a moment think about your desk in your classroom, how have you made it your own? This might be harder if you job-share with someone. When Sonia had a desk in a previous job, she had her mug on it, a small plant and a photo of her family, small things but they felt important. This can be the same for children.

Children's own station/separate space

Some children need their own separate space that they do not share with other children. Often in Reception and Year one classrooms we might see a child having their own station, this is a space where they can retreat to, and work from, it is their space and no one else uses it. Sonia had one child in Year one and his station had a blanket hanging down from the desk, sometimes he needed to retreat under this, he was still hearing what was happening, but he needed time away. Being able to be under the desk, under the blanket, brought him the calm he craved but also enabled him to still be in the room listening to what was happening. Often a child's station will be personalised for them, as mentioned above. Many of the children we work with who have individual workstations have a personalised visual timetable on their desk, sometimes a now and next board too, we described these in Chapter 2 and link to them in Chapter 8.

Regulation zones

A lot of classes now have a regulation zone in their classroom. This is often a designated area with visual reminders for children about how to find some calm and to help regulate themselves, helping them to understand how they are feeling and what is going on in their bodies. There are many different examples of visuals you can use for this, see the OT Toolbox website (n.d.), which has a useful section on zones of regulation, and in our resources Chapter 8 we have an example that you could use. The regulation zone can meet the ideas of a space to react and a space to relax that were mentioned above. Often colours are used in this area, for example, red for rage, and green for calm. In the Introduction, we discussed the pros and cons of narrowing the emotional vocabulary to limited facial images and colours. We still think these tools are useful but in the context of expanding and developing children's language and understanding of emotions and feelings and recognising how they feel in their bodies.

The regulation zone areas only work when children are shown and supported to use them, and this needs to be something which is referred to. Children are supported throughout the year, not just at the start of the year. Ideally, this would be a whole school approach and not just a classroom approach. It is also important that all children know they can use it, this is different to the individual station or an individual child's calm box, the regulation zone area is for the whole class. Below are some examples of what you might have in the space with further examples and recipes in Chapter 8.

Regulation zone ideas

The following are very helpful examples:

- making a space with cushions and blankets to sit on and be cosy
- visual regulation reminders about feelings and emotions and where they appear in the body
- visuals of yoga/movement poses to use
- breathing tools: some examples are finger breathing, bubble breathing, blowing an imaginary candle out, home-made breathing fidget toys (examples of these can be found in Chapter 8), and an expandable breathing ball, which can be bought on Amazon)
- a calming bottle (instruction on how to make one in Chapter 8)
- a quiet fidget toy, such as tangles, homemade slider snake breathing tool, stress ball, stretchy or squishy stress toy
- hand cream to do a hand massage

- images of peaceful, calming spaces, for example, a beach, woods, a waterfall, a garden
- soft material, some children love to feel the comfort of soft material that they can just hold

A space to retreat

We are increasingly seeing classrooms that have a space to retreat within the classroom, this might be a pop-up tent or a canopy/area. This might be separate from the regulation zone and have little in it other than a few cushions and a blanket. It is a space where children can go if they are feeling they need some space or are feeling overwhelmed, it gives them a chance to have a moment out. Sometimes we use these specifically for individual children, but it can also be useful for the whole class and for anyone to use. Children need guidance at the start of the year to know what this space is for, how to use it and to know there is no stigma in needing this.

Lighting

This can be a tricky area to change, but the light in your room can have an impact. Some of our old classrooms and buildings have strip lights, which can be harsh, but some classrooms are very dark and need to have the lights on. Below are some suggestions we have seen work effectively.

- We have seen teachers who have introduced an aromatherapy defuser, which includes a glow lamp which can be set to different colours to alter the mood in the room, the combination of the smell and light helps with this.
- Other teachers use warm white fairy lights to brighten up dark corners or a wall-mounted lamp to illuminate a special set of pictures. You can buy inexpensive animal lights which are battery-operated. Sharon saw a cute light-up bunny in Rabbit class recently, connecting to the class name.
- Mirrors reflecting natural light from windows can be very effective or a wall-mounted light panel which is dressed to look like a window can provide extra light.

- Fish tanks with lights in can also be helpful to add interest and light to an area.

The cloakroom

These are often spaces which can cause a lot of stress. They are often tight spaces with lots of things in them, often these areas can cause conflict. There may not be much you can do with the actual space but a few things might be worth considering.

- If you have a child who finds the space difficult, have them use it on their own, and send them in first before the others go in there.
- Have clearly designated pegs and think carefully about which children may be together in the same area.
- Think about sending one group to pack water bottles and book bags while another group gets their coats, then swap locations, cutting down the numbers of children there drastically.
- Consider making Welly name pegs, if children keep wellington boots in school. It can save lots of time if the children have both boots together, ready to put on, and don't have to search the cloakroom to find their other boot!

The dining area

The dining areas in schools are often very loud, large and noisy. Many of the children we have worked with over the years have found these spaces difficult. Some schools have been able to work on the acoustics by adding material to the ceiling, but in many buildings, this is not possible. Thankfully, some of the new builds in our area have thought about this and they are better spaces. However, if you have children in your class who find this space challenging, there are a few things you could consider:

- Ear defenders can be so useful. Thankfully, they are becoming much more popular and many more children are being offered them and some families are using them to manage overly sensory situations outside of school. I have worked with some children who dislike wearing

them and also some parents who have been reluctant for their children to have them as they don't want them to look different, but with more children using them, this is becoming less of an issue.
- Using another space. For some children, the dining area is too big, noisy, frightening and overstimulating and, even with ear defenders, it is too stressful for them. The next question to ask is, are they able to eat in another space? Some children we work with have their lunch in their classroom with their friends, as the school have managed to find a member of staff who is happy to sit with them before they go outside to play. Other children sit outside in the corridor area, where there is room for a table, again, they have a friend and member of staff with them. Sometimes we hear staff say it is not fair on the other child to be missing out on the dinner hall with lots of friends; one way around this is to have a rota of children/friends who would like to have lunch outside the main area (make sure the child this is for likes the people on the rota and that the additional child wants to be on the rota).

The toilet area

We probably all recognise that the toilet area in a school sometimes can be pretty unpleasant! But it doesn't have to be. A few things can help this:

- *Smell*. This is simple but important, I have a really strong sense of smell and toilet areas in schools can make me feel extremely unwell! This is the same for many children. There are ways around this, it's basic but make sure they are probably cleaned. It might be that once a day is not enough, make sure children flush the toilet, remind children not to wee on the floor and if they do, to tell you so it can be cleaned (sorry, this might sound coarse but when you have worked for a long time in early years, you get used to talking about the basics!).
- *Anxiety*. It is not uncommon for Reception children to have high anxiety around the toilets. We have both worked with many children over the years and we do a lot of work early on helping with this particular anxiety. Some ways to help this are by writing simple social stories about using the toilet. In some schools we have put characters on the doors that the anxious child likes as an encouragement to use the toilet. I have had other children have a laminated photo in their pocket of their

parent as a comfort for when they need to go into the toilet. Sometimes using pictures of comic superheroes or well-known book characters stuck on the toilet doors can soften the space and make it more inviting. Sharon worked with a teacher who would add a small amount of food colouring to the water in the toilet at the start of the day and encourage the children to investigate what colour the water was that morning!
- *Too many people.* For some children the problem they have with the toilet area is other people being around. For these children, you may need to adapt and make sure they can use the toilet area when other children are not present.

The outdoor area

We know that many children who have high SEMH needs can often find learning outside so much easier than learning inside the classroom. Throughout the book we offer ideas that can be used outdoors as well as inside. We recognise that sometimes it is hard to have the child outside when you don't have an additional adult to support them. However, with some classrooms this is possible. This year I worked with a child in Year one, he had his workstation which helped him a lot, but he was a child who was calmer when he was outside. The classroom backed onto the outside space, with large windows to see the outside space. The school made a designated space outside the classroom, which was sectioned off from the rest of the playground. The child was able to use this space at agreed times, to help him relax, calm or re-focus. It was agreed with the child when he was in this space he was not to run off to the rest of the playground, and this worked for this child. If you can make a space like this, here are some ideas of what could go in this space:

- chalk: different-sized chalk, perfect for mark making, making trails etc. on the pavement
- things to make an obstacle course: for example, logs/safe bricks, hoops/beanbags/string/planks/tyres.
- bug finding kit: magnifying glass/pot to put them in, bug-identifying sheet. You could also swap these with bird-/butterfly-/bee-identifying sheets (Sussex Wildlife Trust, n.d.).

- water play: use colour in it sometimes, guttering is a great addition to this and empty squeezy spray bottles
- opportunity to make mud paint/dandelion paint/grass paint
- den-making material, something to hang it over. It doesn't need to be large, it could be for a toy.
- bubbles, with different sized wands: get them to make their own wands. In Chapter 8, we have added our homemade bubble mixture recipe.
- things to make a treasure trail: they could hide some treasure and make a trail/map for friends to find
- materials to make nature art (https://andygoldsworthystudio.com):
- petals, twigs, grass. See if they can create something that they can photograph, it doesn't need to last, the fun is in creating and then changing it.
- area to grow things in: get them to grow some flowers/vegetables. They could grow them and then measure them regularly to see how big they grow. You can grow many different plants in tubs, we regularly grow tomatoes, beans and sunflowers with children.
- clipboard, paper and pens outside: keep them in a tub with a lid on so they are easily accessible but also kept dry
- small world play: you could make a dinosaur land in a tyre. Add sand, pebbles, some twigs, etc./have small world dolls and make a house for them out of sticks, leaves, etc.
- have small cuts of wood and number them, or number pebbles: these can be used in lots of different types of play
- a bigger cut of wood with some nails in it: have a pile of elastic bands and they can stretch the bands between the nails making a pattern
- make skittles out of empty plastic bottles, fill them with rice and number them
- a tub of natural loose parts: pine cones, pebbles, shells, sticks, string, and seeds, these are great for imaginative play

Conclusion

In this chapter, we considered how the environment can affect how children feel and respond. Hopefully, this chapter has given you some ideas about adjustments you can make that will support an individual child and the whole class. If, at the end of this chapter, you are thinking about making changes to your classroom, it is worth having a conversation with the children in your class and finding out what their thoughts and feelings are. If you are making changes, remember to warn them first, as for some children, the change in the layout of the classroom could be unsettling.

 Resources

https://andygoldsworthystudio.com
https://www.pinterest.co.uk/indyflwr/reggio-emilia-classroom/
https://www.reggiochildren.it/en/reggio-emilia-approach/

References

Murphy, K. and Benham, F. (2023) *50 Fantastic Ideas for Supporting Neurodiversity*. London: Bloomsbury.
OT Toolbox (n.d.) https://www.theottoolbox.com/regulation-station-ideas/
Sussex Wildlife Trust (n.d.) Identifying sheets. Available at: https://sussexwildlifetrust.org.uk/discover/go-wild-at-home/activity-sheets/spotting-sheets
TTS (n.d.) An introduction to inclusive practice with Dr Sharon Colilles. Available at: www.youtube.com/watch?v=3m8dLCcGKKk

4 | Sensory Needs

I am currently writing in a shady spot on our camping pitch in the Dordogne, France. I am very aware of the hot dry smell of the earth under my feet and the dappled sunlight filtering through the bright green leaves of the shady trees. The sky is light blue and the sun's rays are illuminating the leaves on the trees to an emerald green. In the background I can hear children laughing, a couple bickering in French as they try to erect their tent and birds twittering. Cooking smells are drifting across to me and making my mouth water and my stomach growl. This is a highly sensory experience which I am fully enjoying and am feeling glad to immerse myself in it.

Each of us have our favourite smells, tastes, sounds, textures and sights which stimulate or calm us. Sonia enjoys cold water swimming whereas I much prefer pool swimming. I love aromatherapy oils and use them daily as part of my skin care routine. The smell is calming, and the feel is luxurious on my face. It is important to each of us that we surround ourselves with things which we know help us to remain calm and happy. However, there are smells, sounds, sights, tastes and textures which we tend to avoid because they grate on our nerves and cause us to feel uncomfortable. I try to avoid polystyrene in packing boxes. The sound and feel of it make me shiver. I am not a fussy eater but I cannot eat certain foods because of their texture rather than their taste.

Take a moment to reflect on things which help you feel calm. Could you make a "calm kit" to keep in school which may help you during times when you feel heightened or overwhelmed?

DOI: 10.4324/9781003467021-5

Imagine having to be in an environment where you felt something grated on your nerves all day and there seemed to be nothing to dilute the uncomfortable feelings to help make them manageable. This can be the experience for some children in our classrooms.

In this chapter I will be particularly focused on some of the signs of sensory overwhelm you may spot in a child in your class. Although a small part of Teacher Training is allocated to SEND (special educational needs and disability), there is limited time to explore things in any depth. Speaking to someone who has just completed their PGCE (postgraduate certificate of education) last week, it was interesting to chat about what might be valuable to include in this chapter without repeating what has already been taught. Following that conversation, I felt it would be useful to consider what the outward signs of sensory agitation are, what the triggers may be, and suggest possible life skills and tools which can be taught to help regulate a child all through their life.

First, it is important to note that some of us simply have sensory preferences. Others have sensory processing disorders. Others may be autistic and find certain sensory aspects completely overwhelming. Sonia and I work as a part of a trauma informed team. We work with children who have experienced some very traumatic events. Trauma can cause a child to have adverse sensory reactions. It stands to reason that if the trauma is sensory, then the solution to the trauma can also be sensory. In her book, *Know Me to Teach Me*, Louise Bomber (2020) talks about understanding behaviour as communication. If you take time out to observe and know the children in your class, you may spot some tell-tale signs of sensory issues for which you could easily provide some relief.

As we are thinking about how a teacher on their own in a classroom might be able to help regulate a child quickly and easily, it is invaluable to have a box of calming tools they can grab from a shelf to use. Always try and make the activity age-appropriate. It might take a few minutes to initially set up the box, but the contents of this box could quite literally save hours in trying to bring a child who is experiencing sensory overwhelm back to a regulated state.

Things Sonia and I use regularly with infant children are sensory rice (see instructions in Chapter 8 on making this), slime, playdough, aroma dough – lemon or peppermint fragrance to pep up, lavender to calm

SENSORY NEEDS

down – water beads, threading beads, and special chews designed for children who put everything in their mouths. On occasions I have worked with children who are biting through electrical wires and have recommended using a heavy duty dog chew which can be kept for the child to use. The specialist chews only last one sitting for these children so it is important to provide something which will last.

All of these items can be quickly grabbed off a shelf to help a child have a moment or two to regulate, calm and get ready to learn again. They are most effective when used with a timer so that the child knows that the expectation is they will rejoin the lesson when the timer runs out.

With slightly older children, jigsaw puzzles, construction toys with instructions to follow to build something specific, massage tools, and even reading a book in a quiet corner can work just as well.

How do you know when someone is experiencing sensory difficulties? This child will find it difficult to sit still on the floor or in their chair. They may push parts of their body hard into the floor, slide their stomach across the surface of a desk, swing on one leg of a chair, chew everything. You may see a child lifting their legs and pushing their knees hard into the desk in front of them. Constantly putting their head down on the desk. Flicking pens or pencils. Tapping, humming, making noises. Fiddling with anything to hand. Sometimes it can look like self-harm – banging their head on things, walking into walls and slamming their body into surfaces to get some sensory feedback. Pulling eyelids hard, biting fingers. Putting chair legs on top of their toes and sitting on the chair so the feet of the chair press hard into their foot. All or any of these might indicate that the child is experiencing some sensory difficulties.

Think about what the behaviour is communicating. Consider what the child is showing you they need. Try and meet the need the child is communicating. For example, if the child is rubbing their stomach across a table, bracing their legs, fidgeting, I would suggest they may be holding a lot of tension in their joints and probably need a movement break to release that tension rather than being offered a chew toy or some sensory rice to play with.

If I saw a child pushing, pulling, biting themselves in order to get some sensory feedback, I would encourage the child to spend some time with sensory rice, playdough, jigsaw puzzle, etc., using the age-related items suggested earlier. We have seen children calm incredibly quickly using both sensory rice or water beads. A memorable experience of this was with a Reception child who flitted from one thing to another and was unable to be still. I was reduced to tears of joy during one session as I watched him sit and play with water beads for 17 minutes without distress or dysregulation. It was the first time I had seen him able to stop, be still, focus, show pleasure and be calm. It was a eureka moment and one which has been repeated since as I observed the power of sensory calming activities during a few moments of play.

SENSORY AIDS

If a child is finding it difficult to sit still, consider if the child can feel the extent of their body. What could help with this?

- A designated space like a carpet tile to mark their area when sitting on the carpet.
- Sitting so they can push their back into a wall or table leg or even on a chair may help.
- A wobble cushion could help provide the sensory feedback they need.
- A fiddle toy would give them permission to move their fingers while keeping the rest of their body still to listen and join in.
- Send the child for a movement break. A sensory circuit or trail can be very effective before sitting for longer periods. These can be very helpful in getting the child ready for learning and in a regulated body state to sit down. It is not helpful to simply send the child to run around the playground. Running in circles increases agitation whereas running between two points, in a straight line, reduces overwhelm.
- Encourage the child to engage in breathing exercises.
- Encourage the child to engage in tensing and relaxing exercises.
- Ask the child to carry out some jobs, e.g. brushing the patio, stacking chairs, wiping tables. All these deep pressure activities will help reduce tension in joints and allow the child to be still and focused for longer periods.

All the activities above are designed to release tension and help the child regulate themselves. In Chapter 8 you will find some handouts for a Toolbox. This is a tried and tested kit which I have found works well with children of all ages in primary school. To start with, the child will need to be taught the strategies, i.e., breathing, tensing and relaxing exercises, etc. However, if this is part of your whole class regulation plan, they will be familiar with these techniques and will be more comfortable using them individually when necessary. Initially the child may need prompting by the teacher to use them by using scripts, such as "I can see you are finding it hard to sit still. I wonder if your body is tense? I think it would be a good time to try some tensing and relaxing exercise. Let's squeeze orange juice" (The orange juice exercise is one detailed in my Toolbox in Chapter 8.) After a while, the child can identify for themselves when they are struggling and will automatically use a tool from their toolbox to help them calm and regulate.

I have also seen these strategies work particularly well for children with a diagnosis of attention deficit hyperactivity disorder (ADHD). They begin to understand and read their body signs and sensations and are able to use the strategies practised to help them calm, focus and engage for longer. These strategies are shared and taught as life skills. They are things which can be used at any age in any situation or any location. The more the children practise them, the more sensitive they become to what works best for them in a given situation.

REFLECT AND PLAN

- How could you invest an hour now preparing some grabbable resources which could save you hours of time calming a child in class and subsequently talking to parents at the end of the school day, sharing with them what has happened for their child during school?
- How can you invest to accumulate regulation personally and for the children in your class?

- If behaviour is a communication, which communications have you misread as wilful bad behaviour which could be explained as a sensory need which the child has?
- Are there certain behaviours which trigger you to become more aware of your own sensory preferences?

The ultimate goal is to help children self-regulate. For some children, this takes time and practice. If there has been trauma, a child may need to grow new neural pathways in order to learn how to successfully deal with a difficult situation or sensory overload. To learn a new skill and grow a new neural pathway takes five hundred repartitions. To master that skill and get to a point where we can use it without even thinking about it takes ten thousand repartitions. That is a lot of practice! These are not quick fixes, and we need to be prepared to support some children for longer than others. However, these are things which we have tried and tested and have had success with over several years of practice. If they work, keep doing them, don't stop. Keep things in place. The Toolbox in something which can journey through school with a child. It is not a short-term fix, these are skills for a lifetime.

CASE STUDY 4.1

I remember working with one child whom I observed found it extremely difficult to get her fingers dirty. We started a graduated approach and I encouraged her to make water handprints on paper towels. We progressed to talc handprints, then used chalk which she tolerated on her hands. We did some baking and used some syrup which she had to push off the spoon with her finger. This was done next to a sink so she could wash her hands immediately or lick her fingers, then wash her hands if she preferred. We used PVA glue during art lessons and I encouraged her to paint her hand and pull the glue off when it set. We were then able to progress to finger painting and hand painting. By the end of this particular project, I remember a very happy child rubbing paint over her hands and forearms and laughing in merriment as she produced an enormous picture on a length of wallpaper on the floor.

As you get to know the children in your class, read their communication correctly and actively try and provide for their communicated needs. Then you will find that the whole class is much more settled and regulated. Your confidence will grow as you try things out and you see what helps certain individuals. You will become proactive in aiding regulation rather than reactive in managing behaviour fallout. This will aid your own regulation and wellbeing too and make for a much happier class environment.

Another Year 5 girl asked for "glue therapy"! This involved taking herself to the back of the classroom, painting one hand with PVA glue, letting it dry and peeling it off before returning to her desk and carrying on with the lesson. She knew those few minutes alone with a sensory activity helped regulate and calm her. Her teacher was willing to be flexible in accommodating and meeting her needs. That child spent less time out of the classroom with members of the senior leadership team (SLT)and more time in class, safe and learning with her peers. She developed a very trusting relationship with her teacher as she knew they understood her, recognised her needs and thought of ways to help.

Conclusion

We can all appreciate how sensory experiences can bring us pleasure or discomfort. In this area sometimes very small changes can make a massive difference to a child who is struggling in your class. Sometimes it may take a bit of trial and error before you discover exactly the right thing to help alleviate an acute reaction to something particular. Encouraging children to practise life skills which will help them to regulate, manage their discomfort and increase their focus is so important. Setting the trajectory of body management and a healthy understanding of the things they struggle with will not only help in your classroom but will provide the foundations for managing for the rest of their lives. This chapter has provided many suggestions of tried and tested strategies which I can genuinely say work when engaged with wholeheartedly. I hope this chapter, combined with the Toolbox visuals in Chapter 8, are a real help to many Teachers and will benefit far more children than I would ever be able to reach in my own work.

Reference

Bomber, L. M. (2020) *Know Me to Teach Me*. Hyde, Cheshire: Worth Publishing.

5 | Transitions

Transitions underpin the majority of our work, as most of the children we work with find transitions tricky. In this chapter, we are going to explore the area of transitions and ways we can support a child through them. Often when we think of transitions, we think of major ones, such as moving class or moving school, and those are significant, but in our work, we also think a lot about small transitions. We are going to look at a variety of transitions from the micro to the macro and suggest several different practical ways you can support the child through the transition.

MOMENT FOR REFLECTION

For a moment think about how you experience transitions, this might sound odd, but transitions affect all of us. We all experience many transitions in a day and throughout a year we may occasionally have major transitions as well. Do you have strategies that help you cope with them? Do you find transitions hard, maybe not the micro but you may find the larger ones tricky?

Micro transitions

Micro transitions can so easily be overlooked, they are small everyday transitions a child can encounter. A few examples are moving from

DOI: 10.4324/9781003467021-6   **61**

the carpet to the desk, going out to playtime, coming in from playtime, lining up for assembly, and changing for PE. These might sound small and insignificant, but some children find them extremely challenging. You may have a child who can cope with some micro transitions and not others. This may depend on their window of tolerance that day, that moment, or it may be a particular micro transition that is always a challenge for them.

Sometimes the micro transition they are struggling with is having an adult near them. For some children with their window of tolerance, their capacity for having an adult near them can be extremely low, sometimes our default is to be physically near the children who are struggling, but sometimes this is the opposite of what they need. Louise Bomber and Daniel Hughes (2013) describe the need for a *dance of attunement*, which can at times involve time together but at other times involves time apart, we can pick up on this by noting the child's body cues.

Examples of body cues from a child indicating that they are struggling could be:

- fidgeting
- no eye contact
- may start to get louder or quieter
- rocking on chair
- looking out of the window
- yawning

How can we support the micro transitions?

Recognise

First is to recognise the trigger, it may be that lining up for assembly is always hard for a child. If this is the problem, consider whether they have to join the line with everyone else, could they do a job until the line is ready to move and then join the end or the beginning if that is more manageable?

Forewarned is forearmed

If you know a transition is coming up that they may find tricky, then forewarn them. Go up to them individually and explain that in 5 minutes the class will be going out for playtime. This is good practice for all children, and announcing it to the class can help many, but for those that you know will find this tricky, also tell them individually.

Visual timetables

These have been mentioned in other chapters and they can be so useful for children who find transitions hard, helping them to know what is coming up and the change to expect. Now and next boards are also useful for some children who find micro transitions challenging. If a child doesn't need the visual part and the now and next is too simple, you could do a mini checklist timetable for them. Have a small whiteboard, with a list of three or four things that they need to do that morning and get them to tick them off.

Is it necessary?

Sometimes we need to ask the question of whether all transitions are necessary. If you have a child who finds it hard to move from the carpet to the table, skip this step, and set up their own station as mentioned in Chapter 3 on the environment. This way, they can work from their station and don't need to move to and fro from the carpet to the table. Or you may have a child who finds going to assembly challenging, do they need to be in assembly? Could they have a job to do while everyone else is in assembly?

Have predictable routines

For children who find transitions tricky, having a predictable routine can make a difference in helping them feel calm. This might include an activity they do each day when they arrive, a job they have to do, such as taking the lunch list to the office or handing out pencils after playtime. If the routine needs to change, where possible, warn them first.

Support

Some transitions have to happen that the child may find difficult, coming in from playtime is often a time children can find hard. If you know this is tricky for them, you will need to put in place additional support for this, as part of the daily plan for that child. As mentioned above, using the pre-warning will help to let the child know the change is coming up. Some tools that can help with transitions back into the classroom are:

- Bring the child back into a quiet classroom before the other children come in. Get them to do a settling job inside, e.g., count ten pencils, or sort number lines for a maths lesson; counting and sorting tasks can be especially regulating around transitions.
- As you bring the child back inside, count the number of windows together as you walk down the corridor.
- Arrange for the child to come in slightly early to do a sensory fine motor activity or jigsaw activity before others arrive.
- Some children find having some responsibility can help them transition. This might be helping to clear up some playground equipment or buddying with a child in a younger class.
- Other children find having a challenge at this time helpful, seeing how quickly they can run to the door, using a timer to time them.

Arriving in the morning

One micro transition that many children find hard is the arrival in the morning. Here are a few thoughts on how to support this.

For some children this is an incredibly tricky time, Sonia has a little boy she supports who finds the entrance time to school too loud and too overwhelming, so he comes into school through the main entrance which is quieter and calmer. Other children arrive slightly later or earlier. In other schools where I work, one or two children arrive and immediately have some time with an adult, often they have something to eat, some breakfast cereal, toast or fruit. It's an opportunity for them to arrive calmly, connect with an adult in a gentle, nurturing way and then they join the class for their day. These small interventions are fairly easy to set up, but they can make all the difference to a child arriving calmly.

CASE STUDY 5.1

Sonia is working with a little boy who finds the transition into school incredibly stressful. He had been arriving sobbing, and when he entered the classroom he started to throw things and break things. The school had changed the starting time for him, so he arrived 15 minutes after everyone else. He arrives at the front desk and a teaching assistant meets him, to calmly welcome him. They slowly walk towards the classroom, doing a discovery walk on their journey, noticing any changes, looking for specific things, some days it might be how many pictures of children they can see, another day it might be how many dinosaurs they can find. Once they get to the classroom they have a calming sensory activity for him to do when he arrives, often playdough or sensory rice. They play with this for around 10 minutes, until the adult thinks he is calm enough to join the rest of the class activities.

Leaving at the end of the day

In a similar way to arrival, consider what the child finds hard, if it is the noise and busyness of everyone leaving, consider if they can leave a little earlier, or from a different entrance. Some children benefit from having 10 minutes with an adult at the end of the day rather than the beginning. One child Sonia supports has some time colouring alongside an adult at the end of the day, she finds the colouring calming and having a calm adult alongside helps to support her regulation.

Job-share teachers

Increasingly we see several job-share teachers in classes, for some children, this can be hard to manage. Sometimes they appear to prefer one person over another, although it is often less about that and more about coping with change. One way to support a child with this is by having a picture timetable showing who is looking after them each day of the week.

This could be on the child's station if they have one, and a copy can also go home with the child so the parent can support them. Some classes also have a page on the door saying. "Today the adults in class are...". They have laminated photos of the adults and velcro to stick the pictures on each day, recognising this can support all children, not just the child needing additional support.

For further reading on this area, the book, *Mental Health and Wellbeing in Primary Education* by Dr Laura Meek, Joanna Philips and Dr Sarah Jordan (2020) has an excellent chapter on daily transitions.

Medium transitions

Medium transitions are those transitions that happen less frequently but still can cause some disruption and unease. Some examples of this are doing a class assembly, school plays, and Christmas parties. We often think that "nice" things that happen in school, such as having a scientist come in to show an experiment or someone bringing animals to show will be exciting and fun for the children, and we don't need to prepare them. For some children, this is hard for them to manage, the surprise of a new person, the change in routine and timetable, the unknown about what the person will bring, and the expectations can be overwhelming and frightening and the child can feel emotionally unsafe. However, there are ways we can support the child in this and here are some suggestions.

A class visitor

As mentioned above, we often think having a visitor bringing something to share with the class can be an exciting part of the day, and they can! However, sometimes children need some additional support around this, a few days before, mention to the whole class about the visit, and, if possible, show them a photo of the visitor and talk about what they will be doing. If they are doing something with the children, briefly explain that to them. If they are bringing something to show, e.g., animals, you might want to show photos of these. With the child that you think might find this tricky, talk to them about this visit on their own, and if possible print out some of the details, for example, the person's photo, with a few lines explaining what they will be doing and maybe some other photos. For example, if it is someone doing science experiments, maybe photos of these. Have a copy of this in school and revisit it with the child, let the child's adults at home know that this is happening and send a copy home with the information, so they can talk to the child about it. Think about where the child will be in the classroom during the visit, will they feel safer at the front or back? Do they need you or another adult near them to check in with them? Is there anything they need to help them feel secure during the visit? This might be a fidget toy or something to hold.

School trip

Often we expect children will love the school trips, but for some children, this can cause anxiety. Some children may have never been on a trip before, and they may not know what this means. Other children will have anxiety around who they are going to sit with on the coach. Which adult will be with them? Will they know where the toilets are? Will they like it? How long will they be away for? What will they eat? When you are doing a school trip, prepare the children well in advance. You will have spent ages preparing for this trip, planning it, doing the risk assessments, include within the planning when you will tell the children. You might want to do this a few weeks ahead. Let the whole class know you are going on a trip and tell them where you are going, then as the trip day gets closer, give them more information, such as how you are getting there, showing them pictures, and looking it up on the internet with them. Some children in the class will need additional support, they will need to know who they are travelling with, and which adults are with them. They may need to look at the details for a week ahead, looking at it each day with a trusted adult. Some schools do social stories for individual children who are doing a trip, one they can look at in school and have a copy to look at in their home, with enough details and photos to help them feel prepared and calm. This kind of detail is for big trips such as to an animal park or museum, but also smaller trips such as a visit to the church or the local library.

Class assembly

Many schools have classes taking turns to do the class assembly and sometimes invite parents to these. I know many teachers who dread these, not just the children! Some children love these and thrive in them, for others, it fills them with dread. You will hopefully know your class well and know what will work best for them all. These events take lots of preparation and this in itself can be stressful for some children. If you have a child who finds this hard, have a conversation with them about what they would like to do in it. If they don't want to be upfront, is there something they can do without being seen? If the event itself will be OK but lots of practising is tricky, minimise how much practice they need to do. You could consider pairing children with someone who brings the best out in them for a dance or song, so they are doing things together and don't feel so alone.

School parties

These usually happen at the end of term, particularly around Christmas or at the end of the school year. There are many children (and adults) who find parties overwhelming, too loud, too unpredictable, too sensory. I am not saying we should ban parties! But we can consider ways we can make them less overwhelming. If you have a child who easily becomes overwhelmed, think about having a breakout space they can go to which is quieter, and calmer. Think about the music you play, if you are having music, and the food you offer, if you are having food. I know it's obvious but lots of loud music, and sugary food make for one major sensory overload for everyone! I think this happens a lot less now than when my children were at school, but I do know some classes/schools where the Christmas party is one big sensory overload.

Moving class

This will vary in every school. In some schools the class moves up every year, usually to a new teacher, I have a few schools I work in with mixed-age classes and the children may stay in class with the same teacher for a couple of years, but, generally, children will experience moving class and teachers several times during their time in primary school. As I write this chapter, it is term 6 and we are about to do move-up day in our area. This is where all the classes move up to the next class for a trial day or half-day and it is the day the new Reception children have a visit and the Year 6s have a trial day in their senior school. This can cause a lot of anxiety for some children; they settle into their class/routine and then they are told it will all change. For Reception children, this can come as a massive shock. Over the years I have encountered many Reception children who presume their school life will always be in that classroom with their teacher. One boy this year wanted to know if I would still be with him at his new school when he is big; on exploring this with him, he presumed I would stay with him until he goes to secondary school and maybe be there too! We can start preparing children for the class change in advance, talking to them about the change at the start of term 6, and, where possible, having the new teacher pop in to meet the class or maybe take a lesson or read a story. Some children will need some additional support around this, with the Reception children we work with, we spend the whole of term 6 helping to prepare them. This term we have been making packs for the new teacher about each child. The children have drawn a self-portrait, made a collage about the things they like, and taken photographs in school of the things they like. These are then shared with the new teacher. This is as much for the child as it is for the new teacher, as it is a gentle way of reminding the child over a few weeks that a change is happening and it is a way of helping them think about a new adult they will need to connect with. We also get the child to visit the new teacher and classroom on errands, taking a note or pen the teacher might need, as a way for the child to make small connections. The teacher makes an effort to look out for the child as they are going around the school, stopping and saying hello, and making small connections. These small details make a huge difference. If possible, we also get the child to visit the new classroom while it is empty, maybe during assembly or their PE lesson. The child can explore the classroom, and notice what is different and what is the same. The other key thing with a child moving class is enabling them to take with them the tools that work. One of my Reception children this year has his own station to work at, and this will be set up in the new class. He also has a calm-down kit, again, which will move with him. His current teacher will do a handover to the new teacher explaining what works for him and what his triggers are.

The new teacher can do some work in letting the children know something about themselves, sharing what they enjoy, e.g., if they have pets. These may sound small things but they can help a child to feel a little more settled. At the start of every year, I use an "all about me bag" with the children I work with. It has a few objects in it about me and what I like doing, I have a knitted swimming doll to look like me, pictures of my family, a few shells and pebbles from the beach and a laminated flower from my garden. This is a simple way of letting children know a little about who I am and what I enjoy. With the photos of my family, I can talk about how one of my daughters lives in Norway, so I don't see her very often. Small details like this can be helpful to children, it can reassure them a little about who this adult is who is about to spend time with them. With some children it can also let them know that all families are different, we don't all live in the same house as a family. For some children that is helpful to see with others too.

New children arriving in the class

Arriving in a class part-way through the year is hard for everyone, for the child who is new but sometimes the rest of the class can find it tricky too. In the next section on major transitions, we will explore moving new schools which will cover how we support the individual child, In this section I am looking at the rest of the class. Where possible, and I know it is not always possible, let the class know ahead of time. Pre-warn them that a new child is arriving, and tell them their name. Talk to the class about how you can all make them feel welcome, ask what they will need, and think about how they might be feeling. For the first few days consider having everyone wear a sticky name label; this is very simple but enables the new child to be able to learn/see the names, and for the rest of the class to remember the new child's name. Of course, this will only work for slightly older children who can read. Some individual children can find the prospect of a new child arriving alarming, maybe worrying. A few years ago I worked with one boy in Year 2, his class had already had five new children arrive that year, and by May, a sixth child was coming in and he'd had enough, he was not impressed and made that very clear. His teacher and the SENDCo spent time with him to think about what would help him. His biggest concern was he didn't want to sit near them, he had his own space, his calm-down kit and he did not want a new child coming near it (he'd had a previous tricky experience about this from a different new child). The SENDCo and the teacher were able to address his concerns and together they came up with a plan.

Change of teacher

For various reasons sometimes staff will change during the middle of a school year. This may be due to maternity leave, a new job, or staff sickness. Changing a teacher during the middle of a school year can be unsettling for some children. Where possible, plan for this, warn the children, have a positive ending of the teacher leaving, and say goodbye. If possible, the class and the teacher should do something nice together on the last day. The teacher can explain to them where they are going, if they are going to a new job, tell them that, if it is to have a baby, tell them they will send a photo when the baby arrives. Some individual children may need additional work on this; for one child we made a social story about the teacher going to have a baby. Ask the new teacher coming in to visit before they start and meet the class, ask the, to tell the class something about themselves, for example, what they like, if they have a pet.

Christmas

Although this doesn't sound like a transition, we wanted to include it here as there are children who find Christmas challenging. Sharon worked with one child over several years who would become increasingly violent between December and March. The child had experienced neglect early on in her life, the Christmas decorations and the dark nights caused her to feel very distressed. Once the staff realised what was happening and understood why this might be, they were able to work with the child helping to prepare her for the changing seasons, preparing for the dark nights and thinking about lovely things that could be done on dark nights at home. As with all of these things, the key is in preparing the child and supporting them with the change. Acknowledge and recognise that a change is happening and this might feel difficult.

Major transitions

This is the area that often gets more thought and time spent on it for good reason big transitions are something for which we all need preparation.

MOMENT FOR REFLECTION

Just for a moment think about what helps you with major transitions. Are you someone who needs time to think through all the details? Do you need to see things to help you, for example, visit the new workplace or spend time in the house before you move?

Sometimes major transitions happen and we are not able to prepare. In the last few years, we have both worked with some children in the looked-after system and sadly sometimes a move happens quickly with no or little preparation. We have also worked with families where they have suddenly been moved to a hostel for safety, but this is or should be unusual, generally, we can prepare children to some extent. Below I am going to look at a few areas of major change that affect a child and how we can support them.

New school

For most children, this will only happen a few times, when they move to primary and when they move to senior, but some children experience lots of moves in school. Reception teachers and Year 6 teachers are often experienced in helping children with this move. If you teach another year group and you have a new child arriving or a child leaving, it is worth asking your Reception and Year 6 colleagues for some tips on how they support children. Knowledge is useful, for the child arriving at the new school and for staff. Where possible, find out a little about the new child, what they like, where they come from, what they find hard, and who they live with. The head teacher should have this information and if they haven't shared it, then ask them for it. You may have the opportunity to meet the new child, and if you do, take the opportunity to find out some key things from the child and family. This will help you when they arrive. For the child, if possible, have a small booklet about the school to hand to the child, some schools have these already prepared. It has a photo of the school, the uniform, a photo of the classroom and playground and the adults in the class with their names, also maybe some other key information. If you have a forest school area or a school/ class pet, put those photos in too. This is relevant for all ages, it is something the child can take home and look at, to remind themselves before they start with you. This is now common practice with Reception classes to send these out before the children start, but there is no reason why we shouldn't also be doing this across the school ages. For the child leaving one school, make sure it is a good ending. You could get the class to make a word art picture for them, using words to describe the child, get the class to make a card for them and take a class photo with them in it. Let them take their name off their drawer, or coat hook if they want to. With some Year 2 children I have worked with this year who were moving to a new school, we made a photo memory book together. They took photos around the school of all the things they wanted to remember and we made it into a simple book for them.

The next few areas are subjects as a teacher you have less control/ influence over, however, you might be in a position to offer some tips to the family.

Moving house

Many children move house. If you have moved house recently, you will know it is often a major source of stress, Sharon has been moving house while writing this book and knows first-hand that it can be challenging for everyone involved! Our first tip around this is if you know a child is moving house, be compassionate and expect they may be a bit wobbly. Even the calmest, most regulated child can have a wobble around moving house. Even if they are not anxious about it, the stress in the family can have an impact. I have known families to move house and not involve the children at all, to the point a child leaves one house in the morning and is collected at the end of the day to discover they are going to a new house! Occasionally this is unavoidable, but if the family tell you they are moving house, it is worth asking if the child knows, and what the child knows and, if they don't know, encourage the family to share this with the child. If possible, spend a bit of time with the child talking about the move, and how they feel about it. Be curious with them, and find out if they have visited the house and what they like about it. If you feel the child needs some additional support around this, maybe you could get them to do some drawings about how they would like their room to look, or maybe they could make something for their new room, such as a poster to put on the door. Some families do a scale plan of the new room to help the child think about how they want their new room to look. The family might also need to think about the things they can't take with them, for example, a particular view through a window they like or a piece of furniture that won't fit into the new place. They might need help to think if there are ways they can capture this and remember it. Some families buy new bed linen for the bedroom and involve the child in choosing it, they might also be able to choose colours for the walls in their new room. However, there are some children for whom a house move is a sad and distressing experience, increasingly, we are working with children where they are having to move into emergency accommodation or a hostel. If this has happened, then be mindful that the child will probably need additional support and nurturing through school and consider if they can get additional support through a social and emotional programme your school may offer.

Change in family situation

There can be many changes in family situations that children encounter, this could be from new babies, splitting up of parents, becoming a blended family, or extended family moving into the home. Other changes that can have a big impact on families are changes in financial circumstances, family illness, a car breaking down and not being able to get it repaired, a parent having a long-term overseas assignment, a parent in prison. With all of these, we don't always get told by the family if something significant is changing for them. I always encourage families to talk to the school/teachers to let them know of changes because it will have an impact on children.

Sometimes we first become aware of this when the behaviour of the child begins to change, as mentioned earlier, behaviour is a form of communication, and children are not always able to find the words to tell us how they are feeling or what they are experiencing. Sharon and I regularly have conversations with schools where we are asked to advise because a child's behaviour has become more challenging or concerning. A first question we always ask is, what has changed at home and in school? I am always encouraging teachers to ask families if anything has changed. One little boy I worked with became massively dysregulated after the Christmas holiday, it was a marked change in him. When the teacher explored this with mum and asked if anything had changed, she mentioned that her partner was off sick and the grandfather was dying. They didn't think the child knew about these things. When we explored it a bit more with the child, he was sad because he hadn't seen his grandad recently and he was confused about why daddy was at home all the time and wasn't going out to play with him. Another area that can have an impact on children and families is the neighbours. We both have worked with children whose families are scared of the behaviour of the neighbours and sometimes have been bullied by the neighbours, Sharon had a child whose family locked their door and shut their curtains as soon as they got home, throughout the year, as they felt unsafe from the next door neighbours. If the child tells you this kind of information, do talk to your school's safeguarding lead about this, as a school, there may be referrals to outside agencies you can support the family with.

As educators, you are, of course, not able to change or influence the family situation the children are in, however, you can support them in school and you can make a difference. A few suggestions for this:

- If appropriate, use social stories with the child, using them both in school and at home.
- Use children's books to help the child understand what they are experiencing is not unique to them. At the end of the chapter we have listed some recommended books for children based on issues. We often use books in early years to explain an issue, but this can also be useful with older children.
- Where possible, give the child time to have an adult they can talk to about what is going on.

- Check in with the child, at the start or end of the day, or beginning of the week, and let them know you are there to support them.
- Give the child the opportunity to express themselves through words, art or music. A Year 2 child I was working with a few years ago was experiencing changes in foster placements which was very unsettling for him. I gave him a sketchbook and some pens, I explained he could use the sketchbook to write or draw whatever he wanted and whatever he was feeling. He used this in school and at home, it transitioned between the two daily. He loved drawing and found a sense of calm in the chaos he was experiencing, using the sketchbook was a small tool in helping him find some calm.

Bereavement

This is a difficult subject, and if currently this feels too raw to read, then do skip this section.

There will be times when children encounter death, maybe through a pet or an elderly family member, but sometimes it will be their parents or siblings. The first thing to say is that there are excellent charities that can offer advice and support to families and education settings, links are given at the end of the chapter. Hopefully, your school has a bereavement policy, I would encourage you to read this before you need to, and if they don't have one, I would encourage you to talk to the senior leadership about having one. Sometimes families will know if someone is dying and will hopefully tell you as a school. If this happens, ask them what the child knows, the language being used and if timescales are known. If you do know this ahead of time, let the child know you are aware of the situation. Let them know they can talk to you, and make sure you do regular check-ins with them. Other times it will be unexpected, it's particularly at these times when the bereavement policy is useful as it can be a shock and the bereavement policy is there to guide you through how the school will respond. Below are a few suggestions:

- Have a named person to link with the child. This doesn't need to be the class teacher, but it needs to be someone the child knows and has a trusting relationship with. Let the child and their family know who this is going to be.

- Check with the family what the child knows and the words the family have used.
- Agree with the family on what the class will know and when.
- Check with the family details such as when the funeral is, and if the child is going.
- Have the named person check in with the child each day, and also let the child know where they can find this person if they need additional time with an adult.
- If you have a pastoral lead in the school who uses Thrive or Elsa, allocate the child to have this additional support. This might be something you put in place after a few weeks or months. In time you may need to consider providing the child with a play/art or music therapist.
- There is a description of bereavement with young children called puddle jumping, This is where a child in a moment can be in the grief and the next moment talking about something completely different. The key is giving children the space to experience grief in their own way, and letting them know they are not alone, you are there for them.

Once time has moved on and when the child moves to different classes, the next teachers must know about the significant bereavement. Let them know the date of the death, and let them know who died. This is important information and needs to move through school with the child. If you have experienced a bereavement yourself, you will know that anniversaries and significant times in the year can be incredibly painful and challenging, and, for children, we may see this in a behaviour change.

At the end of this chapter are the details of organisations and books which may be useful. Working with a child who has experienced a significant bereavement can be hard for the staff also, be kind to yourself and ask for help and support for yourself if you need it.

Conclusion

As mentioned at the start of this chapter, transitions are probably one of the key areas of our work, and when we can support them well, and recognise the difficulties they can bring, it can make a big difference to everyone's day. Spending time reflecting on how the children in your class react to transitions and the small adjustments that can be made could save you a lot of time and stress.

In Chapter 8 is an example of a social story which can be useful to support some of these transitions.

 Resources

Websites

Bereavement: Winston's wish: https://winstonswish.org/
Signposting support: this website tells you what is available in your area: https://hubofhope.co.uk/

Bereavement

Coelho, J. (2019) *If All the World Were*. London: Frances Lincoln.
Crossley, D. (2001) *Muddles, Puddles and Sunshine*. Stroud: Hawthorn Press.
Rosen, M. (2011) *The Sad Book*. London: Walker Books.
Stokes, J. (2021) *You Will Be OK*. London: Wren and Rook.
Teckentrup, B. (2014) *The Memory Tree*. London: Orchard Books.

Mental health and attachment

Dowrick, C. and Martin, S. (2015) *Can I Tell You About Depression?* London: Jessica Kingsley Publishers.
Eland, E. (2020) *When Sadness Comes to Call*. London: Anderson Press.
James, A. (2018) *Looking After Your Mental Health*. London: Usborne Publishing.
Karst, P. (2001) *The Invisible String*. New York: Little Brown.
Percival, T. (2018) *Ruby's Worry*. London: Bloomsbury.

References

Bomber, L. and Hughes, D. (2013) *Settling to Learn*. London: Worth Publishing.

Meek, L., Philips, J. and Jordan, S. (2020) *Mental Health and Wellbeing in Primary Education*. Shoreham by Sea: Pavilion Publishing.

6 Creativity

During the COVID-19 lockdown, many adults discovered or rediscovered how good creativity was for their wellbeing, with many people taking up knitting, crocheting, baking, and playing instruments. This was the same for Sharon and me, Sharon is a talented crocheter, and I knit, and we both bake and enjoy making jams and chutneys. We both use these activities as a way of helping to bring ourselves some calmness. We often use creativity with children in our nurture sessions and, since lockdown, I have been focusing on this a lot more. I realised during lockdown that so many adults used creativity to help bring them some peace, calmness and relaxation and I knew from my work with children that many children found this beneficial also, although they seemed to have less opportunity. Since the return to normal life, a large part of the work I do is creative with children. In this chapter, I am going to explore why creativity is beneficial and how it can help children. This chapter will also share many different creative ideas you can use both for individual children and for whole classes or small groups. These are ideas that both Sharon and I have used many times. If creativity is something you are interested in, look at my book, *Creativity and Wellbeing in the Early Years* (Mainstone-Cotton, 2023).

How does creativity help our wellbeing?

There has been a growing recognition of how creativity supports wellbeing. In 2012, a creativity and wellbeing week was curated in London, organised through London Arts and Health, an organisation that supports artists and health professionals to work with individuals and communities whose wellbeing could be enhanced through creative opportunities (https://londonartsandhealth.org.uk/). The wellbeing week has grown over the years to now become a large annual festival across the UK. This festival collaborates with creative, health and cultural agencies, and takes place at the end of May each year (https://creativityandwellbeing.org.uk/). Many mental health websites talk about how creativity can support mental health, for example, the Mental Health Foundation suggests getting involved in the arts can have a powerful and lasting effect on mental health, suggesting it can help to protect against a range of mental health conditions (https://www.mentalhealth.org.uk/explore-mental-health/blogs/how-arts-can-help-improve-your-mental-health), and it can help some people to manage ill mental health and support recovery. Some people, while engaging in a creative activity, can experience a sense of flow. The idea of flow was originally described by Mihaly Csikszentmihalyi. It is the concept that you can become immersed in whatever you are doing, of course, this is not just relevant to creative endeavours, it could be any activity. The idea is that when you are giving your full attention to something, totally immersed in an activity that you are passionate about, you enter a sense of flow in your mind, where nothing else matters, you are completely in that moment. If you want to learn about this, there is a TED talk from 2004 describing this (Csikszentmihalyi, 2004). I know this is something I experience when I am engaging in some creative activities, I become so focused on what I am doing, that I forget everything else going on around me, and my mind quietens and finds calm.

MOMENT FOR REFLECTION

What creative practices do you engage in? Do you have moments where you lose yourself in these? Do you do these enough? Or would you like to do them more?

How does creativity help children?

In the way that creative practice can help adults' wellbeing, we know through our practice that it can also assist children. Both Sharon and I have seen many times when children can become lost in their creative practice, and we have seen how creative practices can bring moments of calm and stillness to the most agitated children and moments of pure joy to sad children. Similar to how many adults have found creative practice to be a useful tool for them, we would like to enable children to discover that too. The National Centre for Creative Health have issued a paper looking at creativity for health and wellbeing in the education system (https://ncch.org.uk/uploads/page/Creativity-for-Health-and-Wellbeing-in-the-Education-System.pdf). This paper recognises that creativity as part of school life can offer children transferable life skills and support their mental health and wellbeing, helping to improve their future outcomes. However, it also recognises that there is a decline in the provision and arts opportunities in schools across both primary and secondary. The paper describes how studies with children and young people who engaged in creative opportunities found positive effects on behaviour, emotional regulation, building relationships with others and promoting resilience and wellbeing.

No right or wrong way

A key part of using creativity as a tool for supporting a child's wellbeing is that they know there are no expectations, no right or wrong way to do what they are doing. Using creativity in this way is not about making a specific end product, having something that looks a certain way. Sometimes we find in art lessons children can become distressed as they struggle to create something specific. When we introduce creativity as a wellbeing tool, we are encouraging children to learn to enjoy the process of making, exploring and being imaginative, without getting stuck in having to produce something specific. Some children will want to make something specific and have a clear idea in their head, and some may get frustrated when it doesn't look like they want it to, but we can support them with these feelings.

However, for many children, it is the physical activity of doing, exploring and playing with materials that they love and find helpful.

We are going to share a few examples of how we have seen creative practice supporting children.

CASE STUDY 6.1

One 4-year-old Sonia worked with was incredibly agitated a lot of the time, she was finding the loudness and busyness of the class agitated her, and she spent a lot of the time with her body quite rigid. She often frowned. One morning Sonia brought in some clay, the girl was having a particularly bad morning and was very cross. The clay was offered with no instructions, no demands being made of her. Sonia had also brought some feathers and sticks but told the girl she could do whatever she wanted with the clay. She hadn't seen or used clay before, but immediately started to roll it in her hands, she loved the feel of it. She spent over 30 minutes using the clay, and she decided to make a nest and a bird to go in it; very quickly her body began to relax as she used the clay, and she became so focused on what she was doing, that her tongue was sticking out as she concentrated, she was in a state of flow. It was so interesting to watch, and she was good with it, she instinctively knew what to do, and how to use the material. We went on to use clay again several times that year, and when she moved on to the next class Sonia suggested to the adults they provide clay for her.

Other creative methods

A sketchbook

Over the years Sonia has worked with several Year 2 children, who have enjoyed drawing. When I discover this, I buy them a sketchbook and some pens or drawing pencils and encourage them to use the sketchbook as a way to find some calm. We talk about how they can use it to express themselves or to lose themselves in the activity. We talk about how drawing can be a way for them to find some calmness and peace. One girl I worked with was moving to live with a different family member, she was quite worried about the move and sad about leaving the area she lived in and the school there. We talked about the sketchbook as a memory place for her, she could draw things, people and places she loved from here, to help her remember. We also talked about how drawing made her feel happy but also helped her to express how she was feeling and how she can do it wherever she is and whenever she needs it, that skill is always there with her. When she moved, she took the sketchbook with her and the family bought her new drawing materials to use and experiment with.

Construction toys

Several children Sharon has worked with have become very creative with either Lego or K'nex construction toys. They have a small tin of either at their workstation and use the bricks or sticks to create and help them become calm at tricky moments. I watched a Reception child build a vehicle and then adapt it so it was able to transport his favourite superhero. He was able to lose himself in the process of trying to build something which fitted his ideas and aims. It was interesting to note that he did not become frustrated if what he built did not work initially. He seemed to enjoy the process of trying things out, experimenting, finding a solution. The result was unique and clever. Similarly, a Year 5 boy found building with Lego relaxing. He preferred to have a bigger project on the go and was able to dip in and out of creating his finished article over many sessions of creativity. While he was creating, he was dreaming up stories about the people who would have inhabited his creations and he would tell me about them when he had completed his project.

Plants and flowers

Both Sonia and I love to use plants and flowers in our creative practice ourselves and with children. We have spent happy times with children growing peas and sunflowers and have talked about how to care for the plants, making sure they have everything they need to flourish and grow. One of my favourite creative activities is flower bashing where you either provide a child with a pot of flowers or send them outside to collect flowers and leaves from around the school site. By placing the flowers on top of some fabric and gently bashing the flowers with a round stone, you can produce a beautiful flower print on the fabric. The bashing of the flowers can become very rhythmic and steady, and I have often noticed that it mimics a heartbeat. This is very calming in itself but the process of picking flowers, arranging them and producing a print which lasts is a very fulfilling and pleasing activity. Flower and leaf printing is also an activity where I have watched a Year 4 girl use a long stretch of wallpaper to produce a colourful and beautiful pattern which we used to decorate a display board in her school. The more she printed, the more confident she became and the more ideas she had. She asked for extra colours of paint and edged her creation with a repeated pattern. It was something she felt very proud of and wanted to share her creation with others. Another idea is very simply placing double-sided sticky tape onto card and sticking flowers onto it to make a bookmark which can be covered with sticky-backed plastic. The flower bashing activity is a little noisy and could be distracting in a classroom where others are trying to learn but the other ideas are quiet and easily accessible by a child on their own.

CASE STUDY 6.2

Recently Sharon has been teaching a Year 5 and a Year 6 to crochet. Both girls have been using the regulation Toolbox discussed in Chapter 4 and Chapter 8 to help them regulate. As part of a regular wellbeing routine and to help the girls enjoy and embrace sitting still and concentrating, Sharon has introduced crochet as a creative hobby they might like. Both girls have taken to it very quickly and are progressing well. They have sat and focused on new learning for at least 30 minutes which has offered an example of positive focus to use with the girls and transfer to learning situations where they struggle to concentrate. Interestingly, while crocheting, both girls have shared people in their family they will be able to connect with using crochet and seeking help and guidance. Both girls have expressed an interest in progressing to more difficult projects where they can make gifts for others. Not only will this new creative skill help them but it may strengthen their relationships with others too.

How can we use creative practice in the classroom?

The ideas we have offered above can be used very simply with a child on their own, they don't need to have an adult with them, it is simply providing the tools to assist the child. The clay I used in Case Study 6.1 is clay bought from a local potter supplier. I usually buy a large bag of basic clay, this can last for a long time and it is a cheap and sustainable way to buy it. I always thought you could only use this clay if you had access to a kiln, but a ceramics friend assured me that isn't the case, it will dry or it can become wet and you can reuse it. Often our default is to offer children a fiddle toy or sensory tool, and these are great, but we have found the creative tools can offer the same calm too but with a more open-ended nature and, I would suggest, scope to further boost a child's mental wellbeing. The idea behind using creative opportunities with children who are struggling is often not about making something specific, although sometimes that will happen, but more about a way for a child to explore and create in a way which is not right or wrong. There is no fixed agenda here, for some children the art lesson can be stressful as they have to make something specific, but in these creative opportunities, it is about giving the child space to discover, be imaginative and explore without feeling that they have to have an outcome. Of course, creative practice is more than visual arts and includes singing, dancing, storytelling, creative writing, crafts, and music-making. We are aware that many of these things won't work for an individual child to do quietly in their space of the classroom, although we encourage you to think about ways you can bring more of this into your class, if possible. In the next section of this chapter we are going to give you some ideas of how you can offer some creative opportunities that a child could do on their own, although you could also adapt these for a whole class or small groups.

Drawing materials

The materials we provide can make a big difference to children feeling that we value what they create. I know school budgets are tight, but simple things such as making sure the materials we offer work, have lids on, are not broken, are important. This sounds basic, but so often I see drawing materials offered to children that look rubbish, and then of course the children don't feel valued and don't value what they have been given or what they create. Our suggestion is to have a basket of drawing materials that the child can use and have a range of materials in it, we have listed some suggestions below with a mix of the basics to some additional ideas:

The basics

- Good quality felt tip pens
- Good quality coloured pencils with a pencil sharpener
- A few lead drawing pencils with a pencil sharpener
- Good quality wax crayons
- Good quality chalk sticks
- Paper of different sizes and colours

Additional suggestions

- Graphite sticks
- Gel pens
- Pastel sticks
- Watercolour pencils
- Small watercolour paint pack
- Chalk pens
- Paint sticks
- Watercolour paper

Colouring-in sheets

We are adding this as a separate section, as some children (and adults) find colouring sheets very relaxing.

The basics

- Good quality felt tip pens
- Good quality coloured pencils with a pencil sharpener
- Colouring-in sheets

Additional suggestions

- Colouring books
- Gel pens

Small-scale designing/sculpture

In the early years classes, we see a lot of junk modelling, moving up the years and this could be described as designing/sculpting, I would argue this is what we should also call it in the early years. Some children love to design, they are happiest and calmest when they are making models. This might sound like a large activity that could cause chaos, but it doesn't need to be like that, if we explain to the children that from their station/corner of the room they need to keep it small-scale. They do often understand this, and then you can offer them the chance to do it on a larger scale at other times. Some children are not able to cope with this, they become frustrated and angry at their inability to make what they want, but for others, this is the most relaxing, calming activity for them. As with everything else, it is about knowing your children. I have a small plastic arts carry case which has a variety of small-scale materials we can use for this kind of activity, I know of some schools who provide this at the child's station to use when they need it. Below are some suggestions of materials that could be used.

The basics

- String
- Scissors
- Glue sticks
- Toilet roll holders
- Small boxes
- Paper
- Plastic bottle tops
- Tape
- Pipe cleaners
- Corks
- Buttons

Additional suggestions

- Natural materials, e.g., leaves, petals, sticks, seeds, shells
- Wool
- Ribbon
- Lolly sticks
- Feathers
- aterial
- Cotton wool

Clay

I mentioned this above, but I am also giving it a section here. I have found clay to be one of the most calming activities for some children, although there will be some children who hate the feel of it, again, it is about knowing your child. It doesn't have to be expensive, as mentioned above, you can buy a bag of basic clay of around 5kg for around £8.10 from a local potters supplier, there will likely be one in your area. It can be a bit messy, but that is easy to manage, make sure you have a plastic sheet on the table, get the child to wear an apron or old t-shirt and wash their hands afterwards. It doesn't need to cause lots of mess, and it can be easily contained to one table space. If you hate the idea of the mess, then you could use air dry clay, you can buy a small pack of 1kg for around £5 from a local craft shop or online. With both types of clay, make sure the remaining clay is in an airtight bag to stop it drying out.

The basics

- Clay
- Rolling pin
- Plastic mat/table cover
- Apron or oversized t-shirt to protect clothes

Additional suggestions

- Cutters
- Stamps
- Items to press into clay

Printing

For the last few years I have been using printing as a creative tool with children, and this is something that many children can lose themselves in, and it doesn't need to be complicated, expensive or messy. Below are a few simple ways to use printing. The joy of printing is that the child can make something that looks great without needing to have lots of creative skills. For those children who like being creative but feel frustrated with what they make, this can work for them. As with clay, it doesn't have to take up a big space or a long time or an adult, as this can be set up on a station for a child.

The basics

- Plastic mat/table cover
- Apron or oversized t-shirt to protect clothes
- Paint
- Plate for paint
- Paper

Found objects printing

- Plate with a thin layer of paint on it
- Found objects in the setting to print with, e.g., dice, dominoes, paperclip, rubber, number blocks
- Lightly press the objects into the paint then press them onto the paper

Using stamps

- Stamps, and you can make these. Here's a link on how to make them (https://www.kitchentableclassroom.com/wine-cork-stamps-a-diy-stamp-set/) or buy some cheaply
- Plate with a few different colours of paint

Lightly press the stamps into the paint and press onto paper/card/material.

Using natural objects

The basics

- Find natural objects, leaves, flowers, sticks, shells, pebbles
- Sponge
- Plate with a few different colours of paint or paint sticks
- Paper or card

Lightly press the sponge into the paint and then dab onto the object to lightly cover it, then press onto paper/card/material. Or if you are using paint sticks, simply paint on the back of the leaf/flower and print this. You could also try using felt tips in the same way.

Nature pictures

Nature pictures are so easy to make. The artist Andy Goldsworthy is a great source of inspiration for this (https://www.nfschools.net/cms/lib/NY19000301/Centricity/Domain/1251/Q3-Andy Goldsworthy.pdf). The website NF schools has some great examples of his art that you could show to children to inspire them.

The basics

- Found natural objects
- Tray to put them on

Additional suggestions

- Paper or card with double-sided sticky tape or sticky-backed plastic

Make patterns/pictures with the found natural objects then photograph them when they have finished. If you want to keep them, stick the objects onto card or paper with double-sided sticky tape or sticky-backed plastic.

Creative writing

For some children, writing is a trigger and distressing, but other children love it. This is giving them the space to write whatever they want, without the constraints or worry about spelling, or punctuation. This might be nonsense poems, stories, a song or a diary. We can help children with this by reassuring them we won't be looking at it unless they offer to share it, we won't be marking it and they are free to write whatever they want.

The basics

- Paper
- Pens
- Pencils

Additional suggestions

- A notebook to keep their writing in one place
- Gel pens

Crochet/knitting/sewing

This might sound a little strange but some children love to learn to knit, crochet and sew and find it calming. Sonia's daughters are 27 and 25, and they and their friends have all taken up knitting, sewing and crocheting in the last few years. They all use it as a wellbeing tool. One of our colleagues spent a term last year learning to knit with a Year 6 child. Naomi, the adult, didn't know how to knit either, so they both learnt together at the girl's request.

A Reception class Sonia worked with last year introduced sewing, and the children loved it. It helped with their hand/eye coordination and many children found it calming.

The basics

- Knitting needles or crochet needle
- Wool
- Material

- Thread
- Sewing needles
- YouTube link to learning to knit

Additional suggestions

- Variety of wools
- Variety of material
- Variety of threads

Simple jewellery making

Over the years many of the children Sharon has worked with have enjoyed threading to make jewellery. This can be unique and reflect something of the child's personality. The process can be developed over years and become quite sophisticated in its design, depending on the materials used.

The basics

- String
- Chopped-up plastic straws or paper straws
- Pasta tubes

Additional suggestions

- Shearing elastic or leather thonging
- Wooden, plastic or ceramic beads
- Buttons

Mosaic making

Many children enjoy using stickers or glueing paper, card or tissue paper tiles onto a shape to create a mosaic picture. Some children like to randomly stick various colours to build their pictures while others carefully select materials which blend well and produce a patterned mosaic. This can be extremely easy, quick and tidy or can progress to be a complicated and messier process. You can also use this same kind of process for stained glass window shapes using black card and sweet papers of coloured film stuck on the back of the card. Sonia has also bought mosaic pieces in bulk from Amazon and used strong glue to attach these to pieces of wood or tiles.

The basics

- Paper
- Square or circular stickers

Additional suggestions

- Small squares of cut-up coloured paper, tissue paper, foil, funky foam
- Mosaic pieces
- A glue stick or PVA glue
- Strong glue
- A template printed on card
- Mini ceramic tiles
- Deep picture frame
- Tile grout

MOMENT FOR REFLECTION

Looking at the lists above, is there a child in your class who you think might benefit from being creative? If there is, maybe you could have a conversation with them about which creativity opportunities they might enjoy.

Having creative examples around the classroom

One way of helping children to recognise, and be inspired by creativity is by having examples of creative practice around the classroom. This might be through images on the wall, examples of craft in the classroom such as knitted/crocheted objects, small sculptures or clay pieces. Also, have a range of books about art, dance, singers, writers and books of poems. When children can see creative practice around them, it can help to encourage them to try something creative themselves.

Conclusion

Creativity is not always the first thing we think of when supporting a child's wellbeing, but hopefully, this chapter has shared some ideas on how it can be a useful resource and how, for some children, introducing creative opportunities could be an essential wellbeing tool that goes with them through life.

 Resources

Books for adults

Brand, L. (2022) *The Joy Journal for Adults*. London: Bluebird.
Churchill-Dower, R. (2020) *Creativity and the Arts in Early Childhood*. London: Jessica Kingsley Publishers.

Books for children

Barnes, Z. (2021) *Meet the Artist Sophie Taeuber-Arp*. London: Tate Publishers.
Beaty, A. (2021) *Aaron Slater Illustrator*. New York: Abram's.
Brand, L. (2020) *The Joy Journal for Magical Everyday Play*. London: Bluebird.
Curry, P. and Curry, J. (2019) *Parker Looks Up*. New York: Simon & Schuster.

Dorling Kindersley (2009) *Children's Book of Art*. London: Dorling Kindersley.
Verde, S. (2018) *Hey, Wall: A Story of Art and Community*. New York: Simon & Schuster.

References

Csikszentmihalyi, M. (2004) TED talk. Available at: https://www.ted.com/talks/mihaly_csikszentmihalyi_flow_the_secret_to_happiness?subtitle=en&trigger=15s

Mainstone-Cotton, S. (2023) *Creativity and Wellbeing in the Early Years*. Abingdon: Routledge.

7 | Staff Wellbeing

Before I start this chapter, I think it might be helpful to say what I think wellbeing is. There are many different definitions, but one I have created for my work and writing is:

- feeling loved
- feeling safe
- feeling I belong
- loving my self
- feeling good about who I am
- being able to cope with life's difficulties

 MOMENT FOR REFLECTION

Just for a moment take a look at my list and think about whether you agree with this list, if you would add anything, and how it fits with you today.

I started writing this chapter in the Easter holidays 2024; the school holidays are useful for writing books! My family and I have come away for a week to Cornwall, we are staying in a cottage on a tiny cove, the sea is right in front of the cottage. We have stayed here many times before, it feels familiar, safe and nurturing. It might sound crazy that I am writing while I am away, but we have a routine that works for us. My husband is training for a big cycling event, so each morning he goes for a cycle ride; my youngest daughter is writing her final essays for her MA in medieval studies, so she is writing for a few hours each morning, and I start my morning with a coffee, a walk along the coastal path and then I come back and write for an hour or so. We then go out for the day, I swim in the sea and we explore and rest. I am writing this to show that nurturing our wellbeing looks different for everyone. What is important is knowing how it looks for you and what works for you. I am sitting writing in the window overlooking the sea, hearing the waves crash on the shore. I can write at home and I mostly do, but I have learnt there is something about being away and writing that I find really productive. I know this experience will boost me for weeks; each day this week I will swim in the sea, it won't be for long, but the cold water is the best stress relief I know.

For me, staff wellbeing is the subject I am most passionate about. I really believe the only way we can do our jobs in education and do them well is if we know how to look after ourselves and how to look after our own wellbeing. In the Introduction, I wrote about how many of the children we work with have a low wellbeing, I really believe we can only support this and boost it if we have good wellbeing ourselves. In this chapter I am going to share with you some ideas, thoughts and suggestions based on things I use and I have seen others use. Wellbeing is talked about a lot more now, however, it can sometimes come across as being something frivolous that rich people or celebrities indulge in, something which will cost money and take lots of time, and, let's be honest, most of us in education don't have a lot of spare time or money! My hope is this chapter will show you wellbeing is not about money and time, there are a few things we can do which can support our wellbeing. I also believe that what underpins supporting our wellbeing is self-love, when we take time to stop, eat well, and look after ourselves, these are important forms of self-love.

The first thing to say before we start discussing the area of staff wellbeing is that I am not a mental health specialist; this chapter is not about serious mental health difficulties. Of course, we can all benefit from looking after ourselves, but if you are really struggling with your mental health, adjusting your diet and doing a hand massage are not going to provide you with the help you need. If you are feeling mentally fragile, then please do seek medical help, go and speak to your GP, or if a GP is not the route you want to follow, please do reach out for help from agencies who specialise in mental health. I have put links in the Resources at the end of this chapter.

The way this chapter will work is a bit like a menu, there are different things on the menu, some of them you will be familiar with and you would like to try again, some will be new and you might be willing to give it a go, and others are just not for you at all, and that is fine. Read through the chapter and see which bits of the menu might be good for you today or this week/month.

MOMENT FOR REFLECTION

Before we start this chapter, I would like you to think for a moment about the last week and ask yourself what you have been doing to nurture your own wellbeing. Maybe you have been exercising, or maybe you have been resting a lot, maybe you have cooked yourself some good meals. Or you may realise that this last week there hasn't been a lot of self-nurture happening. Whatever your conclusion is, don't be hard on yourself, just recognise where you are at.

In this chapter I am going to explore a few categories for wellbeing:

- physical wellbeing
- emotional wellbeing
- spiritual wellbeing
- supporting colleagues

Physical wellbeing

Food

Before I continue this section, I want to acknowledge that for some people food can be a difficult area, many people have a relationship with food which they find problematic, maybe through the types of food or cutting out food or over-eating. If this is something which you think might be a hard one to read, please be kind to yourself. We want this book to be supportive and not one that makes you feel guilty. If you need support with food issues, there are links at the end of the chapter.

We all know that we need to eat well and healthily, but I know for many in education this can be a real challenge; we may feel too busy, too tired to focus on this. Some people can manage without breakfast, but many can't, although I know many staff who find they don't have time to eat breakfast in the morning as the mornings are such a rush and there is so much to do, especially if you have a family to sort out before you get to work. If you are someone who needs to eat breakfast but doesn't have time, could you take something with you to have when you arrive at work? There is a growing recognition that we need to learn to understand our own bodies and what we need, and this will change over time.

Gut health

Tim Spector is a leading voice on food issues and is part of a research team looking at how gut health supports our wellbeing (Geddes, 2022). He has written several books, his latest one, *Food for Life* (Spector 2022), explores how our gut health is closely linked to our physical and mental health. He and his team have been researching how we can improve our gut health, they are big fans of fermented foods. I need to admit here that I am struggling with this! Our boss, Ed, is big fan of fermented foods and I keep trying but I am not yet won over! They have also found that we need variety in our food, and they suggest that we should be aiming to eat 30 different plant-based foods a week. When I first heard this, I was slightly alarmed and thought 30 sounded a lot, but it's not as hard as it might first appear. Thirty different plant-based foods include seeds, nuts, pulses, herbs and spices, whole grains, as well as fruit and vegetables. When I started to think about the coffee beans, chamomile tea, oats, berries, pulses, herbs and spices, nuts, fruit and veg I had each day, I realised that I was usually managing this by the middle of the week. Hugh Fearnley-Whittingstall (2024) has just published a recipe book titled, *How to Eat 30 Plants a Week*. It is full of affordable, simple recipes which ensure you get to eat 30 plants a week.

Ultra-processed food

An area that has received a lot of attention recently in this area is ultra-processed food. Dr Chris van Tulleken is one of the leading voices about this. It is now understood that there is a link between the more ultra-processed food we eat and serious health conditions such as heart disease, cancer, type 2 diabetes, mental health conditions, dementia and poor gut health (van Tulleken, 2023). This can be a baffling area to look into, but the basic tip is ultra-processed foods usually contain lots of additional salt, fat, sugar and industrial chemical additives. Have a look at the ingredient list, if there are long lists and things on there that you don't recognise, it is probably ultra-processed food. When you start to look into this, you realise that many foods are classed as ultra-processed, the obvious ones are ready meals, but also many breakfast cereals, energy bars, tinned soup, diet bars, cakes, biscuits, crisps, yogurts with added flavours, processed meat, such as sausages, bacon, ham, and many shop-bought breads. The advice is to minimise the amount of ultra-processed food we eat and try and eat more fruit and vegetables, dried fruit and nuts, wholewheat bread and oats, pulses and legumes (such as chickpeas and lentils), fresh meat, fish and eggs (unless you are vegetarian or vegan), plain or natural yogurts, tea, coffee and water, or herbal teas. Just to add here, food in cans, such as beans and tomatoes, and frozen food, is processed which is OK, but they are not ultra-processed. I think this is an important area to think about but I am also really aware this can be seen as a middle-class luxury. We all know that many of the ultra-processed foods are cheaper, and this is so wrong. It cannot be right that it is cheaper to buy a six pack of crisps than a six pack of apples, which sometimes happens. I do believe that food is a political issue and one that should be taken seriously by our politicians. I am also aware that for many people having time to cook from scratch, possessing the knowledge of how to cook from scratch and having the money for this can all feel like a luxury. Jack Monroe is a food writer and anti-poverty campaigner who specialises in budget recipes, these are based on her lived experience of living on £10 a week to feed herself and her son. She has written recipe books but there are also free recipes online (https://www.bbc.co.uk/food/chefs/jack_monroe).

CASE STUDY 7.1

Sonia often has conversations with the staff she supports about wellbeing and how they are doing. She has noticed over the years that several staff, often younger staff, mention they don't have time for breakfast or lunch, but they are also finding by the end of the day they are exhausted. Together they have thought about how it might be possible to fit in a least one of these meals, thinking about what would make it easier, what food they could bring in, what they could buy in their weekly shop to easily eat at work, or whether they could bring in leftovers from their meal the night before.

If food is an area you want to think about a bit more, there are some further links and reading at the end of the chapter in Resources.

 MOMENT FOR REFLECTION

Just for a moment think about what you have eaten in the last few days, see if you can add up how many different plant-based foods you have had. There is a *Guardian* article by Linda Geddes (2022) about this.

Exercise

We all know that exercise is important, the NHS guidelines state that adults need to do at least 150 minutes of moderate intensity activity a week or 75 minutes of vigorous activity (https://www.nhs.uk/live-well/exercise/physical-activity-guidelines-for-adults-aged-19-to-64/). Examples of moderate intense activities are brisk walking, riding a bike, hiking, water aerobics, dancing. Examples of vigorous activity are running, swimming, riding a bike fast or on hills, football, rugby, netball, hockey, aerobics, or martial arts.

Research has shown how exercise can reduce our risk of major illness, such as heart disease, cancer, and type 2 diabetes. The NHS website suggests it can lower risk of early death by 30 per cent (https://www.nhs.uk/live-well/exercise/exercise-health-benefits/).

There is a growing problem in the UK with many people being less active. This is often attributed to the change in our jobs, with many jobs being less physical, using cars more, greater use of technology. I would also add to that a feeling of lack of time. I know many in education who feel they don't have time to fit in exercise, particularly when they have families to care for. Once they get back from work, and sort the family out, the idea of also exercising is one thing too many. I really get this, and that was me for a long time. I only started exercising once my daughters were teenagers. The suggestion is to be able to fit it into a routine, so it becomes habit-forming. I found this worked for me; around 11 years ago, I took up swimming, but realised it would only work if it became a habit. I started swimming five days a week early in the morning. I have always been an early riser so it was fairly easy to get up and swim early. I am at the pool for 6.20 and home again by 7.20. This gives me time to swim for 30 minutes before breakfast and sort out my morning routine.

Exercise and cost

I know that sometimes cost can be a prohibitive factor for people exercising, such as gym membership or personal trainers. Thankfully there are exercises that are free, such as walking and running and also there are now many free exercise classes online. In the further information section I have put a few links. Julia Bradbury has written a book called *Walk Yourself Happy* (2023). This book explains how walking can have a massive impact on our mental and physical health and it's free, all we need to do is step outside our house and walk, even for 10 minutes a day, this will make a difference.

Exercise and mental health

As well as exercise being important for physical health, it is increasingly being recognised as important for our mental health. It's linked to improving sleep, managing stress, managing symptoms of depression and anxiety, helping brain and memory function. In 2022, there was a trial in 11 areas with GP practices prescribing walking or cycling to people with some form of mental illness, as a way of supporting their mental health (https://www.gov.uk/government/news/walking-and-cycling-prescription-trial-funding-allocations-published). There is more information on how exercise can support mental health on the mental health website (https://www.mentalhealth.org.uk/explore-mental-health/publications/how-look-after-your-mental-health-using-exercise).

Find your own thing

I think the key with exercise is find your own thing, find what you can do, something that you enjoy. I think to make exercise a habit, it needs to be enjoyable. It might take a while to find your thing, and it doesn't matter what it is. It might be boxing, dancing, roller blading, netball, Zumba, hiking, cycling, pole dancing, acrobatics. Whatever it is, find it, do it and experience some joy. For me, the discovery of cold water swimming has been a massive boost to my wellbeing. I had been enjoying pool swimming and, as I mentioned, that is my main form of exercise, but around 8 years ago I started to cold water swim and was hooked, I now swim all year. Sadly, I don't live near the sea, if I did, I would swim daily in the sea, but I have become very good at finding cold water spots near me. I regularly swim at Clevedon Marine Lake, often on a weekend. I travel to the coast when I can and until the recent flooding I was swimming in Bath Lido, which is a cold water pool in the winter. In the summer I swim in the river, as long as there hasn't been any sewage pollution. It's not for everyone but for me, it is fantastic.

MOMENT FOR REFLECTION

Just take a moment to consider if exercise is the bit of the menu that is for you. Maybe you would like to try something new, or maybe you would like go back to something you have done before.

Sleep

Sleep is an area that often raises the most conversation when I deliver this training to staff teams. It is not uncommon for a lot of people to comment in these sessions that they feel they don't get enough sleep. The question is, how much sleep do we need? Everyone is different but generally it is suggested that most adults need at least 7 hours sleep a night. Some people can manage on less and others need more. I work best if I get around 8 hours a night. Here is a link to the Sleep Foundation who have a table with ages and hours of sleep needed, this is also useful as a guide for children (https://www.sleepfoundation.org/how-sleep-works/how-much-sleep-do-we-really-need). I know that many of the children I work with don't get the recommended amount of sleep.

Why do we need sleep?

Regularly having enough sleep is essential for our wellbeing, as having enough sleep enables our bodies and minds to recharge. It helps our minds to function well and our bodies to fight off disease and remain healthy. Researchers now understand that if we regularly don't get enough sleep, it may suppress our immune system, increase heart conditions and high blood pressure and risk chances of type 2 diabetes. It can also lead to depression and anxiety. I know if I don't have enough sleep, I find it very difficult to get through my day. My ability to think clearly, make decisions and to generally be patient and kind with people is massively diminished due to lack of sleep. There are many things that can impact our sleep, if you are a parent with young children, a carer, or experiencing the menopause, you may find that your sleep is impacted regularly. Also stress can be a contributor to trouble with sleeping.

Recommendations for getting a good night's sleep

There are some things we could do to aid our sleep, although I am aware if you are waking regularly due to caring needs, this is a trickier time. If you are struggling with sleep due to menopausal issues, you might want to consider HRT (hormone replacement therapy), I found this helped me a lot.

There are a few general tips that can help most people:

- *Sleep pattern*: Sadly the idea of catching up on sleep in the holidays or on weekends is a myth, the ideal is to try and go to bed and wake up at the same time each day.
- *Natural light*: Try and get at least 20 minutes of natural light, if possible in the morning. Scientists have found that morning light can improve alertness, boost energy levels and mental ability and improve our sleep. Katherine Latham (2023) has written an article in the *Guardian* explaining how the light levels affect our circadian rhythms.

- *Good sleep hygiene*: This is about making sure your room is dark and cool to sleep in. Not having distractions in your bedroom, such as a TV. Avoiding electronics with a screen for at least an hour before you go to bed. This is linked with the blue light we get from the screens. This blue light suppresses melatonin which is a crucial hormone for sleep. Also screen time can be stimulating to the brain, helping us to be more awake. For more information on screen time and the impact on sleep, see the Calm website (https://www.calm.com/blog/screen-time-before-bed).
- *Avoiding alcohol, nicotine and caffeine before bed*: These are all stimulants and help to keep us awake. You may find that alcohol makes you sleepy at first, but it can also act as stimulant and impact your sleep during the night.
- *Bedtime routine*: I am always recommending bedtime routines for children and it is the same for us. A few suggestions are having a bath or warm shower before you go to bed, reading or listening to a book, drinking a warm drink, such as a herbal sleep tea, using lavender on your pillow, using a mindfulness sleep app to help you go to sleep. The composer Max Richter has written a 8.5-hr piece of movement to sleep to, it is an incredible piece of music, sometimes I use this to help me sleep, you can find it on Spotify and Apple Music (https://www.maxrichtermusic.com/albums/sleep/).

If sleep is an issue

If you find that you are regularly not getting enough sleep, and this is concerning you, it is worth speaking to your GP about this.

Emotional wellbeing

Stress

We are all aware of stress in our lives and the impact it can have on us. Stress is not all bad, we need some stress to help us get up and get out to work in the morning. However, too much stress can be so harmful. Before I continue with this section, I want you think about how stress impacts you.

MOMENT FOR REFLECTION

How does stress affect you? How do you know when you are stressed? What are the signs for you and where do you feel it in your body?

The above questions are important for us to consider, stress does show itself in our body, sometimes through our moods, or we might feel it in our stomachs or necks, we may get headaches or feel it through a racing heart. There are many ways our bodies let us know we are too stressed, but we are not always very good at listening to this and actioning on it.

A few years ago I listened to an Unlocking Us podcast with Brene Brown. She was interviewing the authors Emily and Amelia Nagoski, whose book is called *Burnout: Solve Your Stress Cycle* (Nagoski and Nagoski, 20209) (https://brenebrown.com/podcast/brene-with-emily-and-amelia-nagoski-on-burnout-and-how-to-complete-the-stress-cycle/). Their book is full of many helpful ideas and suggestions. One of the main take-aways for me is their suggestion that we all experience stress daily and we need to release it daily. They created a menu of ideas of how we might release this stress daily:

- time in nature
- spending time laughing
- spending time crying
- engaging in a creative practice
- exercise
- connection with others
- affection: 6-second kiss, 20-second hug

The suggestion is to spend some time doing one of ideas from the list to help you release the stress each day.

Time in nature

There's growing research around how time in nature can support our wellbeing and this can significantly help to lower our feelings of stress. Some of this research has come from Japan, they have a phrase called shinrin yoku, translated into English as "forest bathing". The idea of shinrin yoku is to walk slowly through trees, not rushing, noticing the smells, the colours, the sounds around you. One of the leading writers and researchers on this is Professor Yoshifumi, who has written a book, *Walking in the Woods* (Miyazaki, 2018). In this book he explains the science behind their research. You may not live near wooded areas, but we can all get the benefits of being outside, just by stepping outside of our workplaces or homes. We are fortunate in the UK that we have many green spaces, our towns and cities have parks and green areas, even walking down residential streets, we will find trees and flowers. Below are a few suggestions on how you could add some more nature to your life:

- *Grow some food or plants*. You don't need to have a garden for this. If you wanted to grow food, you could grow some things from a pot on a window sill, such as herbs and salad leaves. Growing herbs and using them in food would also add to your 30 different plants for your gut health! Growing house plants is a really easy way to bring some greenery into your home. Many are easy to grow, the big tip is don't over-water them. Around January–March you can often buy pots of bulbs in the UK, such as tulips, daffodils, or hyacinths. Put these on your window sill and you quickly will have beautiful flowering spring flowers.
- *Bring the outside in*. You can do this all year round. This might be through buying flowers, having holly in the house at Christmas, picking a twig of early catkins in the winter, collecting conkers or autumn leaves and putting them in a bowl in your house.
- *Find places near you where you can spend time in nature*. There is something wonderful about spending time in nature in wild spaces, but most of us are unable to do this very often. As I mentioned at the beginning of this section, we are fortunate in the UK, we do have many green spaces around us. You probably have local green areas that you use, but there may be some wonderful spaces near you that you are not aware of. There may be allotments you can walk through, or church graveyards; that might sound odd but they can often be great mini-sanctuaries of nature.
- *Exercise outside*. This can be a great way to get the nature boost plus the exercise we all need. Whatever your exercise thing is, see if you can sometimes do it outside. For a while I went to a yoga class and in the summer we often had the lessons outside, and there was something wonderful about hearing the bird song, feeling the sun while trying to

do the yoga poses. For me, the greatest joy is when I can swim outside. As I am writing this section, I am in the Lake District while my husband is taking part in a big cycling challenge. I am swimming each day in lakes and in the sea, while trying to write a bit as well! Being in the cold water with the view of a mountain is magical.

Self-compassion

I think the area of self-compassion can be one of the most powerful parts of supporting our own wellbeing. Self-compassion is about how we are kind to ourselves, how we love ourselves, how we speak to ourselves. Kristin Neff is a writer and researcher in this area (Neff, 2011). I first discovered a TED talk she did, and I found it so helpful (www.youtube.com/watch?v=IvtZBUSplr4). For a long time I had a critical inner voice, I would speak to myself and criticise myself in ways I would not do to anyone else. Kristin suggests we need to create a kind and loving inner voice. She proposes using scripts to help us practise using kind words to ourselves. When I first heard this, I worked really hard on it and now mostly my critical inner voice has gone. I have found this practice particularly helpful when I have been going through extremely stressful situations, either with work, home or health concerns. I often gently tell myself that I can get through this, it is OK to be finding it hard, my body is amazing and will come through this. Brene Brown in her book, *Atlas of the Heart* (Brown, 2021), encourages us to have large and rich emotional vocabulary so that we can fully understand how we are feeling and what we are experiencing. She suggests if we have a limited range of emotion words, we are less able to understand what we are experiencing and less able to be compassionate to ourselves.

> **MOMENT FOR REFLECTION**
>
> How do you speak to yourself? If this is an area that you think you could work on, one exercise you could try is to write yourself a letter, offering words of encouragement and love, as if you were writing to a friend or a loved one. You don't need to share it with anyone, but keep it to one side for a time you might need to read it.

> **A SIMPLE SELF-COMPASSION EXERCISE**
>
> Before you move on, you might like to try this simple self-compassion exercise. It is one I use on all my adult wellbeing training sessions. Find some hand cream, and simply take a moment to stop and give yourself a hand massage, taking time to pay attention to what you are doing. You may like to speak to yourself gently and kindly as you do this, or quite simply the action of taking time to stop and gently do a hand massage is an act of kindness and compassion to yourself. I often suggest teachers have some hand cream in their classroom, when they are feeling tense or stressed, they take a moment to do a hand massage, it will help to lower their stress response.

Spiritual wellbeing

You may think of spiritual wellbeing as being only for those who engage in faith practices, but I think we can all engage in practices that support our spiritual wellbeing, whether we have a faith or not. There are a few areas I am going to suggest that come under this category.

Experiencing silence and stillness

As someone who mostly works in Reception classes and nurseries, I am aware that my work environment is often very noisy, and maybe because of this I often crave some silence at the end of the day and on my days off. Some people find that having times of silence can help to lower their stress levels. It doesn't need to be for big chunks of time, although I have friends who have done silent retreats and found them to be extremely helpful. You could choose to have some time when you don't turn on the radio or TV, going for a walk without listening to music or a podcast can give you the chance to hear the sounds of nature.

Yoga and mindfulness

Many people find these practices hugely beneficial, particularly for helping to lower stress levels. There are many different types of yoga and many classes you can attend in person or online. In the further information section I have put some links for meditations, apps and yoga online. Many think that mindfulness meditations require lots of sitting still for ages, they can be more varied than this! I have used mindfulness a lot over the years, and at times of high stress I have found it to be so helpful in bringing some calm, I'll often sit in my greenhouse and do a mindfulness meditation; that might sound strange but for some reason that works for me.

Gratitude practice

Many faiths encourage a practice of gratitude. Brene Brown (2021) has some interesting research on this. She has found through her research a link between people who were joyful and having a gratitude practice. Her research showed that having a daily gratitude practice invited joyfulness into their lives. Many people find this practice useful and it doesn't have to be linked to a faith. Dr Julie Smith (2022) also advocates this practice as a useful part of our self-care tool kit. A gratitude practice can help us to reframe our thinking, it can be easy to get stuck on the negative parts of life. But if we think for a moment about the things we are grateful for, it can help to reframe the picture and let us move on for a moment from the negative. I use gratitude practice at the end of the day, usually before I go to sleep I will think of three things I am grateful for that day. They don't have to be big things, it might be the swim I have had, having a meal with family, seeing the red kite fly over the garden. I also use gratitude practice while I am outdoor swimming, often saying to myself how grateful I am for the swim, for the feeling of the water, and how my body can cope with the cold, although if it's very cold those thoughts happen at the end of the swim as during the moment, my mind is taken up with how cold it is!

Supporting colleagues

Acts of kindness

Supporting colleagues is not only good for their wellbeing but it is also good for our wellbeing too. On the Mental Health Foundation website their CEO Mark Rowland proposes that being kind and compassionate to others also supports our own wellbeing (https://www.mentalhealth.org.uk/explore-mental-health/kindness/kindness-matters-guide). There are simple ways we can do this, making a drink for someone, offering to do their playtime duty if you can see they need a break, sharing a cake, fruit, or chocolate in the staff room, bringing in flowers to the staff room. Sharon and I work in a team of makers and creatives, because we are peripatetic, we only see each other at a team meeting around once a term, but when we do meet, there is always food to share, cakes that have been baked, jams or chutneys that someone has made and other times soap and balms that others have made. We often leave the meeting with something that one of the team has made, this always feels like a nourishing and nurturing way to show kindness to one another and feel loved by our team.

Checking in with colleagues

In the busyness of a school day and when support staff are on limited hours, it can be easy to forget to check in with one another. Many of the children we work with have teaching assistants to support them, these are poorly paid jobs, on limited hours to support our neediest of children. Staff doing these roles can feel isolated, sometimes they are outside of the classroom spending lots of time with the child on their own, and sometimes they experience aggression, violence, and high emotions. It is so vital we check in with staff, make sure they are OK, most days they will be fine, but not always. It is so important that everyone in a school has people who are making sure they are OK, supporting them, checking in on them.

Wellbeing toolkit

In our team we all have our own wellbeing toolkits. These are not always physical things but they are reminders of what helps us, we have all individually created them with items or ideas that we know help us. We would suggest you make one too. Below is an example of what is in Sharon's Toolkit and in mine.

Sonia's wellbeing toolkit
- Coffee first thing in the morning
- Chamomile tea throughout the day
- Swimming costume (both for pool and wild swimming)
- My garden
- Connection to friends and family
- Books
- Creating something

Sharon's wellbeing toolkit
- Tea and quiet time with my husband first thing
- Essential oil skin care which smells wonderful
- Singing
- Feeding the fish in our pond
- Time just looking out at fields and hills near our home
- Pool swimming
- Crocheting
- Reading

Conclusion

We can only look after children and support their wellbeing if we are in a good place ourselves. We hope that this chapter has offered you a few ideas to reflect on. When I am delivering wellbeing training, I introduce it as a menu, there will be things that you are attracted to and want to give a go and others that you don't like, and that is fine. We hope that this chapter may give you a ideas and few more insights. Looking after our wellbeing is not a luxury or frivolous act, it is essential.

 Resources

Food

Fearnley-Whittingstall, H. (2024) *How to Eat 30 Plants a Week: 100 Recipes to Boost Your Health and Energy*. London: Bloomsbury.
Five ways to identify ultra-processed food with Chris van Tulleken. Available at: youtube.com/watch?v=uAVuU2xS_YA
Getting started with the 10 principles of intuitive eating. Available at: https://zoe.com/learn/intuitive-eating
How to identify ultra-processed food and what to eat instead. Available at: https://zoe.com/learn/what-is-ultra-processed-food
Jack Monroe recipes. Available at: https://www.bbcgoodfood.com/recipes/collection/jack-monroe-recipes

Exercise

Couch to five. Available at: https://www.nhs.uk/live-well/exercise/get-running-with-couch-to-5k/
Joe Wicks. Available at: youtube.com/channel/UCAxW1XT0iEJo0TYlRfn6rYQ
NHS exercise classes. Available at: https://www.nhs.uk/conditions/nhs-fitness-studio/
Yoga with Adriene. Available at: https://yogawithadriene.com/

Sleep

Smiling mind app has some sleep meditations on it. Available at: https://www.smilingmind.com.au/smiling-mind-app
Walker, M. (2018) *Why We Sleep*. London: Penguin.

Stress

Chatterjee, R. (2018) *The Stress Solution: The 4 Steps of a Calmer, Happier, Healthier You*. London: Penguin.
Smith, J. (2022) *Why Has Nobody Told Me This Before?* London: Penguin.

Time in nature

Allen, R. (2022) *Grounded: How Connection with Nature Can Improve Our Mental and Physical Wellbeing*. London: Mortimer Books.
Bradbury, J. (2023) *Walk Yourself Happy*. London: Piatkus.

Stillness and silence

Kagge, E. (2018) *Silence in the Age of Noise*. London: Penguin.
Maitland, S. (2009) *A Book of Silence*. London: Granta Books.

Yoga and mindfulness

Buddhify app. Available at: ttps://buddhify.com/
Smiling mind app. Available at: https://www.smilingmind.com.au/
Williams, M. and Penman, D. (2011) *Mindfulness: A Practical Guide to Finding Peace in a Frantic World*. London: Piatkus.
Yoga with Adriene. Available at: https://yogawithadriene.com/

References

Bradbury, J, (2023) *Walk Yourself Happy*. London: Piatkus.
Brown, B. (2021) *Atlas of the Heart*. London: Vermilion.
Fearnley-Whittingstall, H. (2024) *How to Eat 30 Plants a Week: 100 Recipes to Boost Your Health and Energy*. London: Bloomsbury.
Geddes, L. (2022) Interview: Go with your gut : Scientist Tim Spector on why food is not just fuel. Available at: https://www.theguardian.com/lifeandstyle/2022/may/15/go-with-your-gut-tim-spector-power-of-microbiome
Latham, K. (2023) Why you should make the most of the extra daylight when the clocks change. Available at: https://www.theguardian.com/science/2023/mar/19/spring-forward-why-you-should-make-the-most-of-the-extra-daylight-clocks-go-forward
Miyazaki, Y. (2018) *Walking in the Woods*. London: Aster.
Nagoski, E. and Nagoski, A. (2019) *Burnout: Solve Your Stress Cycle*. London: Vermilion.
Neff, K. (2011) *Self-Compassion*. London: Yellow Kite.
Smith, J. (2022) *Why Has Nobody Told Me This Before?* London: Penguin.
Spector, T. (2022) *Food for Life: The New Science of Eating Well*. London: Penguin.
van Tulleken, C. (2023) *Ultra-Processed People: Why Do We All Eat Stuff That Isn't Food and Why Can't We Stop?* London: Cornerstone Press.

8 | Resources

This chapter is designed to be a helpful resource bank of things for you to try, make and do. The idea is that things are easy to follow, photocopiable and hopefully will save you time hunting for various things we have referred to in previous chapters.

I (Sharon) must admit that Pinterest is my best friend when it comes to hunting for resources. I have tapped in various search criteria and found a wealth of lovely activities and ideas which have helped me when working with children. I would recommend a browse. By typing in 'Sensory Activities', you will be faced with all sorts of suggestions, some of which will capture your imagination and play to your interests and strengths. There are lots of really good ideas and many activities which have already been thought out for you. It saves a lot of time and energy just tapping into resources which are already available rather than reinventing the wheel.

Ideas we have shared below are from our resource banks and have been used successfully with children over our years of work. It is only a taste of things for you to try but we hope it will be enough to help you get started and discover what works best for the children you work with. There are a mixture of sensory activities and recipes, regulating exercises, an example of a simple social story and the visuals for the regulation Toolbox described in Chapter 4. We would encourage you to have a look through and think about the things you could introduce for your class or individuals which may make a big difference in the way they experience school each day.

Sensory activity ideas

Bubble mixture recipe

Ingredients

> 1 cup of strong washing-up liquid (it needs to be Fairy Liquid or similar, eco ones don't work)
> 6 cups of water
> 1 tablespoon glycerin

Instructions

Mix it all together, this makes excellent bubbles and can be used with giant bubble wands.

Playdough recipe (from the Imagination Tree website)

Ingredients

> 2 cups of flour
> ½ cup of salt
> 2 tablespoons of cooking oil
> 2 tablespoons of cream of tartar
> 1 cup of hot water

Instructions

Mix everything in a bowl, stir it well until it forms a dough, knead it and then play with it. You can add food colouring, essential oils, or leaves such as lavender or mint into the water.

Cloud dough recipe – make with the child

Ingredients

2 cups of cornflower
1 cup of hair conditioner
Food colouring, if desired

Instructions

Mix everything together, by hand, in a bowl. I like to use very cheap raspberry conditioner which gives a mild fragrance and colour to the dough so there is no need to add food colouring. This keeps in an airtight box for about 2 to 3 weeks.

Fake snow recipe

Ingredients

2 cups of bicarbonate of soda
¼ cup of tea tree hair conditioner

Instructions

Mix ingredients together in a bowl. You can use any light coloured hair conditioner but I have found that the tea tree tingle cheap hair conditioner makes it feel and smell cold. Get a small digger or some snowy animal toys, a spoon and some small snowflake-shaped cutters to play in the snow. You can mould this snow, so can make a snowman or snowballs with it. It fits nicely into a plastic tray and will last about 2 weeks.

Sensory rice

Ingredients

Half a bag of rice
1 tablespoon of paint
1 tablespoon of water to loosen the paint

Instructions

Pour the rice into a very large plastic zip lock bag. Add the paint and water, mix and seal the bag. Rub the paint though the rice until it takes on the colour of the paint. If the rice needs to be darker, add a little more paint solution. Tip the coloured rice onto a tray and allow it to air dry. When it is dry, break up the clumps and store in a tin. The rice sounds better in a tin! You can mix different colours of rice or add extra things to the rice if you like … glitter, oats, foil shapes, lavender flowers, rose petals, gems, essential oil. Use to play in with toys or prepare a treasure hunt where small items are hidden under the rice for the child to find. Many children simply enjoy the sensation of the rice trickling over their hands. One little girl Sonia worked with enjoyed standing in the rice and have it trickled over her toes. Incredibly, I have never experienced a child throwing the rice which I imagined could happen. However, it does escape the tin as the child plays so it may be worth putting a cloth on the table to catch the stray rice ready to pour back into the tin when you are ready to tidy up.

Ice play

Ingredients

Water
An appropriate container to freeze water in either an ice cube tray or a plastic container

Instructions

- Freeze plastic animals like penguins or polar bears in some ice. Provide the child with a small hammer and see if they can release the animals.

- Blend a little powder paint into the water prior to freezing and use the ice cubes to paint with.
- Make a large block of ice. Colour salt with food colouring or chalk dust. Put it into salt shakers and let the child make coloured patterns in the ice with the salt.
- Put ice into the water play area along with slices of fruit to be discovered by infant children.
- Make ice art. Collect berries and leaves from nature. Arrange them in a shallow dish. Before freezing add a piece of string to hang the creation on a tree outside.

Water play

Ingredients

Water – cold or warm
Large water container so a child can play in it. A washing-up bowl is good for an individual child to play in
Additional ideas of things to add to the water in instructions

Instructions

Some children love water play and find it very calming. You can make the water warm or cold. Use jugs and containers or add bubble bath and get the child to blow bubbles using a straw. This will encourage the child to perform a long exhale breath. A long exhale helps to slow down the chemicals racing around the brain, reduces the heartbeat and helps the body to regulate and calm more quickly. Some younger children don't like breathing exercises whereas others love them. If you have a child who will not engage in breathing exercises, the idea here is to trick them into performing that long, slow blow-out using play to help. I often add dinosaurs or mini My little ponies to the bubble bath and get the children to give the toys a bath.

Breathing

Here are some additional breathing activities and exercises you might like to try with your class. The purpose of these is to interrupt the chemical flow of cortisol and adrenaline around the brain, slow it down, reduce the heartbeat and aid regulation faster.

Breathing is a regulating tool we all use either consciously or subconsciously throughout our lives. By practising this, the children will be learning important life skills which will help them regulate wherever they are at any time. I often remind children that they may not have a fidget toy with them but they will always have their hands and their breath and their body can be used to help them calm.

Pipe cleaner breathing stick

Ingredients

Pipe cleaner
Beads

Instructions

Loop the end of the pipe cleaner, and add the beads onto the pipe cleaner, when you have enough loop over the end so they don't fall off. You move the beads along as you take a breath.

Jellyfish breathing craft

Ingredients

A paper plate
Felt pens
Various colours of tissue paper cut into long thin strips
Sticky tape
A piece of string or ribbon to hang
Hole punch

Instructions

Cut a paper plate in half and get the child to draw on eyes. Turn the plate face down on the table and stick different strips of tissue paper tentacles onto the jellyfish using sticky tape to secure them. Punch a hole in the centre top of the plate and thread through the ribbon to hang it. Hang it up so the child can blow on the tentacles to see how many they can get to move. As they get better and move more tentacles, ask them to stand further away from the jellyfish before they blow. The jellyfish can be left somewhere accessible in the classroom so the child can be sent to blow on it throughout the day.

Finger breathing

Hold your left hand out in front of you, with fingers splayed. Using your index finger on your right hand slowly trace around your thumb and fingers. As your index finger moves up each finger, breathe in, and as your finger moves down each finger, breathe out. Make sure this is completed at a steady pace which allows a long exhale of breath on the downward strokes.

Hot chocolate breathing

This is particularly popular with younger children. Get the children to hold an imaginary bowl of hot chocolate in their hands. Encourage them to give it a sniff, then blow it cool. Repeat this five times by the adult giving the instructions and ensuring the blow-it cool is longer than the give it a sniff.

Petal breathing

Sit in a relaxed pose with your hands facing upwards on your legs. Bring your finger tips together so it looks like a flower with its petals closed. As you breathe in, slowly allow the fingers to open. As you breathe out, slowly bring the finger tips back together again, as if the flower petals are opening and closing. Repeat five times.

Bee breathing

Take a big breath in and cover your ears with your hands. As you breathe out, make a buzzing noise and see how long you can keep the noise going. You can feel the vibration of the noise through your body and some children find this very comforting. The more you practise this, the longer the 'buzz' will be. Boys particularly like this exercise as it can be made into a competition to see who can make the longest buzz.

Box breathing

You can do this sitting or standing. Imagine you are in a small box and you are going to push against the sides of the box. Begin with your hands side by side against your chest, palms facing away from you. Breathe in deeply, then breathe out and push your hands forward, straightening your arms as if you are pushing the front of the box. Breathe in again and bring your hands back to your chest. Breathe out and press your hands to either side of you, each one pushing one side of the box to your right and left. Breathe in again and bring your hands back to your chest. Breathe out and push your hands above your head, pushing the top of the box. Breathe in again and bring hands back. Breathe out and press your hands down below you to push the bottom of the box. Repeat this two times.

Fidget toys

All fidget toys have the potential to become a distraction to the child, others and yourself. I would suggest that all fidget toys need to be under adult control and children may use them only with an adult's agreement. I have found if a child is misusing a fidget toy, a useful script to use is, "By using it like that you are showing me you have had enough and want me to take it away. I don't want to take it away if you haven't finished but if you play with it like that, that is what you are asking me to do. The choice is yours." This puts the responsibility on the child as to whether they can keep the toy or not. I have also found some fidget toys can be used for very specific situations like assembly but do not need to be used at other times. Here are a few ideas of things which might be helpful.

DIY fidget toy

Ingredients

- String or cord
- Beads
- Keyring

Instructions

There is a link with full instructions and pictures on Pinterest at the end of the chapter. Link the string over the keyring, Thread the beads onto the string.

You use this as a fidget toy. This could be something you make with the child and they could make one for school and one to take home.

Calming bottle - ideally make this with the child

Ingredients

1 empty plastic drinks bottle
Items to put in it – sequins, glitter, beads
Clear liquid soap
Glue for the lid

Instructions

Fill the bottle to 3/4 full with warm water
Put the items into the bottle
Top up the bottle with the liquid soap
Glue the lid on

You can use this as an aid with calming breathing, take a breath as you shake and gently breathe out as you watch it settle. Use it to link with feelings of agitation inside your body.

Discovery bottle

Ingredients

1 empty plastic drinks bottle
Rice
Small items for the bottle, e.g., Lego figures, dice, beads, buttons, Playmobil, dinosaurs

Instructions

Lay out the small items on some paper and photograph them, then laminate this to record what is in the bottle.

Put the small items in the bottle then add rice to fill it. The child twists the bottle to see what they can find, they can match them to the photo.

Rice stress ball

Ingredients

> Old sock
> Dried rice or lentils
> Funnel
> Needle and thread to sew up or an elastic band

Instructions

Use the funnel to fill the sock with the rice or lentils, the more you fill it, the firmer it will be. Leave space at the top to tie the end, sew it or use an elastic band. This works just like a stress ball you would buy. Ideally, make this with the child. I have used two white socks to make a snowman using permanent markers to draw a face and buttons. The child was keen to put it in the microwave to see if it heated up. They made their own "hottie" and thought it was hilarious that a snowman could be hot and not melt!

Water bead stress ball

Ingredients

> 2 balloons
> Water beads
> Wide-ended funnel or cut-off plastic bottle

Instructions

Soak a small amount of water beads overnight in water. Roll one balloon longways so it can be inserted into the other balloon. Wiggle the internal balloon about so it is sitting neatly inside the outer balloon so you have a double skin. Insert the funnel into the mouth of the inner balloon and fill with water beads. You can tie off the two balloon mouths together. As an alternative, replace the water beads with flour for a different kind of fidget toy following exactly the same process.

Lavender squish

Ingredients

Dried lavender flowers
Small muslin bag

Instructions

Fill the bag with lavender flowers and tie up the bag.

Resources for regulation

Calm box ideas

This can be a box you have generally in your classroom which is available for all children to have access to or you might want to make a box for an individual child. I have seen both systems used very successfully in schools in which I work. Teachers will often notice when a child is becoming fidgety, loud and unsettled and will suggest they use a timer and have a five-minute brain break using the calm box to help their body become ready for learning again. Things you might put in a calm box are:

- playdough
- squishy ball/stress ball
- small liquid sensory timer
- fiddle toy
- bubbles
- soft material
- lengths of wide silky ribbon

- lavender squish
- yoga cards
- feathers
- head or foot massage tool
- pipe cleaners (good for bending and twisting)
- hand cream for hand massage
- calming bottle
- discovery bottle
- kinetic sand
- slime
- clay
- small tub of Lego
- small tub of thread and beads/buttons
- a slinky toy
- a seed bag
- emotions stones or cards
- fluffy pompoms
- bubble wrap
- a resistance band to go on chair legs

Zones of regulation resources

Zones of regulation are used in many schools in which we work. They help to develop an understanding of emotions and help children to express how they are feeling. A colleague of ours has written a school regulation policy based on the zones of regulation in place of a behaviour policy. This was introduced at the school she previously worked at and was so successful that other schools are now using her 'Emotion framework' as the basis of their own behaviour policy There are lots of free visuals available at: https://www.socialthinking.com/zones-of-regulation/free-stuff, which will help your class manage and understand their own and others' emotions better.

RESOURCES

Regulation Toolbox visuals

The regulation Toolbox was introduced in Chapter 4. The idea is that these visuals are a reminder for the child of things they have talked about or practised with their class and teacher and know will work to help them regulate. They can be printed off and placed in a small box on their desk which can be accessed with or without the prompting of their teacher. It is a tool which can follow them through school. The beauty of it is there are many things they can do from the toolbox while sitting at their desk. If something is working, encourage the child to keep doing it. We have a tendency to stop interventions when we think things have improved. Unfortunately, emotions don't work that way and we can all find ourselves in a tricky place at any moment and may need some help to feel calm. I fully realized this when my husband had a serious accident. My daughter told me after the event that initially what I was saying was incoherent. I thought I was communicating effectively but noticed people were responding to and talking with my daughter rather than me! In that moment of anxiety and stress, I completely lost the ability to communicate clearly with anyone. This made me appreciate how children might respond when they are distressed, agitated and dysregulated.

The Toolbox is a reminder of lots of life skills children can build to help them regulate throughout their lives anywhere and at any time.

Why a toolbox?

- The spanner depicts tensing and relaxing exercises where we can tighten or loosen the body up.
- The multi-headed screwdriver is used as an analogy for breathing exercises. It's the same tool but has lots of different ways you can breathe, much like swapping the head of the screwdriver.
- An allen key is often used to reduce pressure in radiators. Sorting out problems can be a real pressure point for some children. There are ideas shared on the card which could help reduce that pressure.
- The rule book has all the instructions in it. Use this to talk to the children about the need for rules and think about why the rules are in place:
  - Is the rule to keep us safe?
  - Is the rule to make things fair for everyone?
  - Is the rule to help us be successful?

  Get the children to consider which rules fit one, two or even all three categories. I have found when a child understands why a rule is there, they are much happier about keeping the rule.
- The spirit level is to help children think about if they are calm and thinking straight. If they are upset or angry, their thinking brain will be offline and not responding properly. They cannot think, respond clearly or make sound judgements until they are calm and their thinking brain is online again. This is why it is so important to allow children space and time to regulate after an incident. It is no good trying to talk to them immediately afterwards as they will not be in a place to understand and respond appropriately.

Source: Freepik

Copyright material from Cooke & Mainstone-Cotton (2025),
"Help! What Do I Do Now?", Routledge

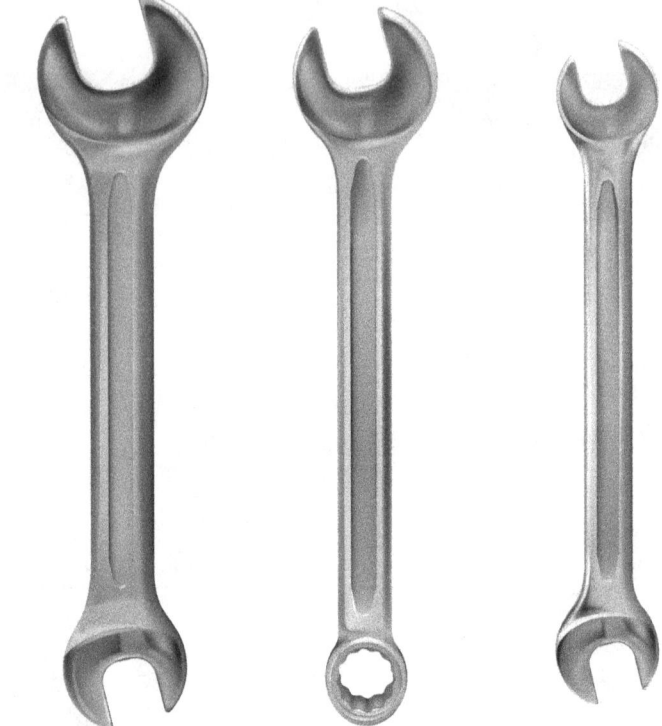

Source: Freepik

Tensing and relaxing exercises

- Squeezing orange juice (repeat five times)
- Curl toes up in shoes, hold for five minutes. then release and relax (repeat five times)
- Sitting on a chair, push legs hard into the floor. Hold for five minutes, then release and relax (repeat five times)

These exercises will release tension from your body and help you to focus, concentrate and be ready for learning.

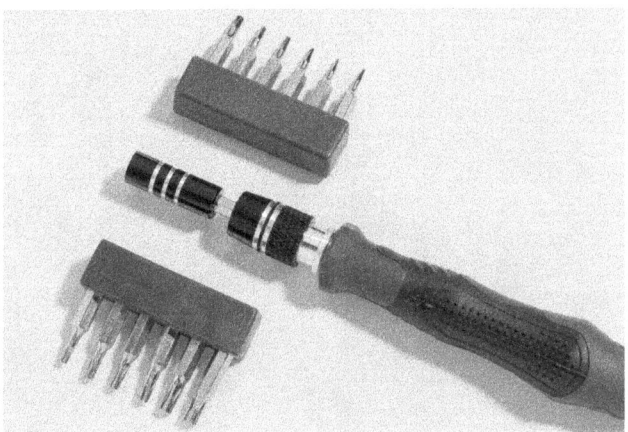

Source: Freepik

Breathing

- Finger breathing
- Petal breathing
- Hot chocolate breathing
- Bee breathing

Breathing deeply introduces more oxygen into your bloodstream. It also slows down the chemicals which are racing around your body and helps you feel calmer.

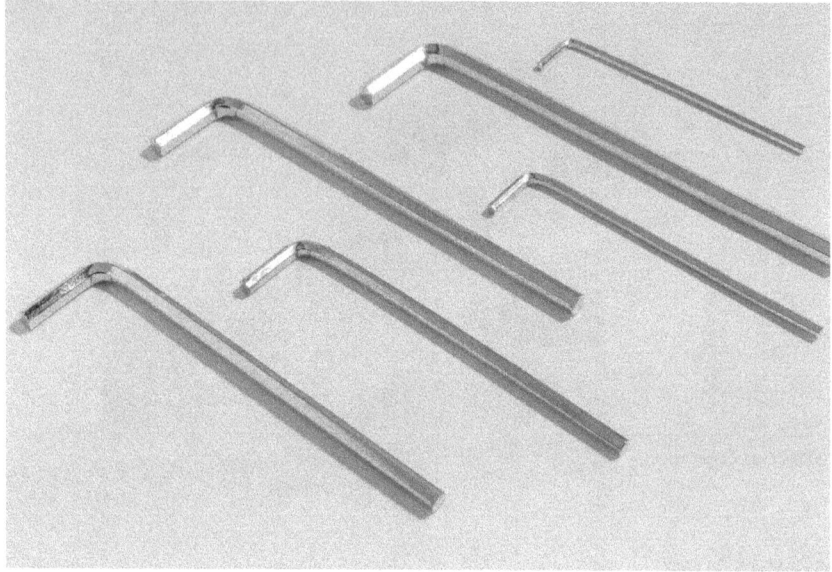

Source: Freepik

Sorting out a problem

- Talk to an adult
- Step away and calm
- Ask yourself – what will happen if I do this thing or that thing?
- Which option has the best outcome?
- Will I get into trouble?
- Ask an adult for help

It can be tempting to try and sort out problems on your own. Sometimes this can make even more problems. Try and STOP! THINK about your options and ACT on what you have decided. Adults are in school to help you problem-solve.

Source: Freepik

Following the rules: why are rules important?

Rules are there to…

1. Keep us safe.
2. Make things fair.
3. Help us be successful.

Think about the rule you are struggling to follow. Which sort of rule is it, 1, 2 or 3? Some rules fit category 1, some fit category 2, others fit all categories! If you understand why the rule is there, it helps you to keep that rule in future. If you cannot decide about a rule, ask an adult to help you decide where it fits.

Source: Freepik

Am I thinking straight?

- If I am angry or upset, I will not be able to think clearly.
- Is there a tool in your Toolbox that could help you feel calmer?
- Is there an adult you could ask for help?

Do not decide to react to something until you are sure your brain is online and you are thinking straight.

Tensing and relaxing and bilateral brain exercises for individual or whole class regulation

Tensing and relaxing exercises can help release tension which is being stored up in the body and waiting to burst out. You can observe this when a child is twitchy and there are big body movements. Often they can fling their arms or legs about and this can be when others get hurt. It is not always intentional but their body is so busy and fizzy that they get to a point that they cannot stay still or fully control their movements.

Bilateral exercises are a good way of getting the left and right hand sides of the brain communicating well. By crossing the body and performing rhythmic motions, this can bring a sense of calm, relaxation and regulation.

These simple activities can be practised at school individually or in a whole class setting and at home with parents/carers and are good regulating exercises which children can learn to use independently.

Butterfly hugs

Cross arms across the chest as you hold shoulders with hands so you are giving yourself a hug. Take deep breaths and tap your hands on your shoulders, alternating right and left hand like the wings of a butterfly.

Let's squeeze orange juice

This exercise can be carried out just using your own body or squeezing playdough. Hold your hands out in front of you, palms turned upwards as if you are holding an orange in each hand. Say, "Let's squeeze orange juice" in a rhythmic way, squeezing with alternate hands, pretending to squeeze all the juice out of the oranges. Repeat this four times.

Tense and relax fist breathing

Open your hands in front of you, palms up and fingers facing away from you. Take a deep breath in. As you breathe in, close your hands into fists. Clench the fists tightly for three counts while holding your breath, then breathe out slowly while relaxing your hands up again. Repeat this five times.

Tensing and relaxing legs and feet

Sit on a chair placing the soles of your feet flat on the floor. Relax your body. Take a deep breath in and tense your thighs, calves, curl your toes up and hold this position tightly for three counts while holding your breath. Then breathe out slowly as you relax your legs and feet. Repeat five times.

Chair press-ups

Sit in a chair. Place your hands on either side of the chair and push upwards lifting your bottom off the seat of the chair. Hold for two or three counts. Repeat five times.

Body percussion/drumming

Use a steady heart beat and tap first the right foot, then the left foot, stamping several times right and left alternatively. Then tap each knee and repeat. Add to this by tapping the chest, tummy, head, cross hands over the body and tap opposite shoulder. Use alternate hands so it is like you are walking up the body with your feet, then hands.

Who's the strongest?

Working with a partner, face each other and link fingers. Person A needs to pull their partner's hands apart while Person B needs to push their partner's hands together. Each person needs to brace their legs in order to remain as strong as they can be. Count down from 3 to 1, then start! Keep trying for five seconds, then relax. Repeat this three times. After three repetitions, put your arms by your side, take a deep breath in for four counts, hold for two counts and exhale for six counts. Repeat breaths three times.

I have seen all of these exercises work for different children. They will find that one or two are better for them than others. It is a case of experimenting and exploring what works best for them, then encouraging them to use them as part of a daily routine.

Tension Tapping Technique (TTT)

Tension Tapping Technique (TTT) is a type of first aid, self-help technique that has proven helpful in calming emotional responses related to stress and traumatic experiences. There is a link at the end of this chapter in Resources which will take you to a short cartoon where the figure taps on certain pressure points around the body. I have seen this activity used in a school every day when the children come back to class after lunch. The video link I have shared is put on the whiteboard and the children and adults join in together. Many children struggle more in unstructured times. They don't understand that the rules in the playground are different, and they may not be so familiar with the staff on the playground. This can lead to difficulties arising and it is often a hot spot in the day when the children transition from the playground into the classroom. TTT can be used as a whole class activity which spills over into individual use as the child becomes more accustomed to using it. I cannot explain how it works but can say, from my experience, that it does. It can become part of the class daily routine at times when children find things most difficult.

Movement breaks

For some children, regular timetabled movement breaks will be essential to help them focus and sit when they need to. I have shared some exercises which can be carried out at the desk but some children need something more with bigger, deeper pressure exercises. One sheet I have shared at the end of this chapter has a different movement for each letter of the alphabet. One Year 5 boy I worked with, who had a diagnosis of ADHD, would be sent just outside the classroom door into the corridor where the movement break poster was displayed. He would use the poster exercises to spell out his name then return to the classroom ready to sit and learn. This worked so successfully that the teacher noticed an increase in his ability to work with others calmly and focus and engage in lessons better.

I have also shared a link in the Resources to a great explanation on sensory circuits with lots of activity specific to the various sections that a sensory circuit leads a child through: alerting, organizing and calming. Sonia and I have experienced great success with these and found that they really help some of the children who find stillness and concentration most difficult.

Social story idea

A social story can be used with a child when they have calmed following a specific incident. I worked with a boy and wrote this simple social story for him. He wanted to be a good friend but ended up hurting lots of his peers, resulting in many of the children in his class becoming afraid of him. Every time there was an incident, he would go to calm in a quiet area of the classroom near to his trusted adult. Initially she would read the story to him when he was calm enough to hear it. After a while he knew the story and was able to read it himself to reinforce what he should and could have done.

As the child gets older the stories can become more sophisticated and can deal with very specific events or times of the day where the child struggles. I remember writing a social story for an older child about the routine of getting ready and leaving school. This really helped him to know what order to do things, gave him permission to get his coat at a quieter time when the cloakroom was not too busy and noisy, and helped with the handover to his parents which was very difficult.

However old the child is, it is important to include how their behaviour will affect others and make them feel. It is also important to let them know what behaviour you are expecting to see. Name the behaviour you are seeing so that it is very clear to the child what you are supporting them with.

I can be a good friend

Source: Freepik

Being a good friend means that I am kind to others

Source: Freepik

I let others go first sometimes

Source: Freepik

I share toys
I play fair
I take turns
I use kind words
I listen to others
I respect other people's space

Source: Freepik

I try not to get too close to anyone or touch someone who doesn't want to be touched.

To be a good friend there are some things I must NOT do:

I must NOT hit

I must NOT poke

I must NOT push

Source: Freepik

I must not put my hands on anyone in any way that might hurt them. If I do, they will feel hurt and sad

Source: Freepik

I want to make my friends feel happy!

Source: Freepik

Copyright material from Cooke & Mainstone-Cotton (2025), *"Help! What Do I Do Now?"*, Routledge

I can be a good friend

Source: Freepik

Visual timetables

Some of the best visual timetables are available on Twinkl back to school hub. At https://www.twinkl.co.uk there are various age-appropriate timetables available and they can be reproduced for use with individuals who need to know when one activity is ending and you are starting another activity.

Now and next boards

This can be as simple as drawing two pictures on a whiteboard to using a laminated sheet with individual laminated pictures which mimic the class visual timetable. For older children, it is good to provide a tick list of the day, so they can tick off each lesson and playtime as it finishes. This helps them to know where they are in their day and how long it is likely to be until lunchtime or going home time.

Fine motor activities

While fine motor skills will improve a child's ability to mark make, they also distract the brain, make the child concentrate and can help them calm. I have mostly used these activity ideas with infant children but have occasionally introduced challenge games with older children too. I often have two jars of pompoms and two clothes pegs. I empty the pompoms onto the desk, set the jars at either end of the table. I set a minute timer, and we compete to see who can pick up the most pompoms and put them in the jar using the peg. I have printed animal shapes or initials of their name on a piece of white paper and asked a child to fill it in with dots using a cotton bud and some paint. I have used hooped cereals which are threaded onto pipe cleaners to make bird feeders or sorted and threaded beads, cotton reels or threading pictures. There are so many ideas and resources on Pinterest for very quick and simple fine motor skills which may also be of interest. I have found that these are often good activities to start the day with. The child anticipates the activity, engages in it, calms while doing it and is able to transition smoothly into the day. Children are able to engage in these activities on their own very easily and do not necessarily need supervision, if you choose the activity wisely. Just because these activities are often aimed at toddlers, it does not mean they are not helpful or worth exploring with older children.

Conclusion

We have shared lots of ideas in this chapter to help you in your quest to manage and regulate your class. Many of these ideas can have a huge impact on a child and will be a lifelong activity they can draw on in times of stress. It is very rewarding to know you have introduced something to a child, helped them to regulate and encouraged them to persevere in order to master and maintain a way back to calm throughout their life journey.

 Resources

Alphabet movement break poster – your-name-workout-kids-680x900.jpg (680×900) (730sagestreet.com)
Cloud dough – https://pin.it/1Gz6UlgGM
DIY fidget toys – https://www.pinterest.co.uk/pin/443182419602422084/
Fake snow – http://pin.it/7qXMC3yEE
Fine motor activities – 100+ Fine Motor Activities For Kids – Happy Toddler Playtime
Playdough – https://theimaginationtree.com/best-ever-no-cook-play-dough-recipe/
Sensory circuits – 0218-Sensory Circuits-Info for teachers-April 2018 (cambscommunityservices.nhs.uk)
Tension Tapping – www.selfhelpfortrauma.org
Visual timetables – https://www.twinkl.co.uk
Zones of regulation – https://www.socialthinking.com/zones-of-regulation/free-stuff

RESOURCES

YouTube videos

- Cosmic Kids Yoga
- Just Dance Kids
- Jump Start Jonny – https://www.jumpstartjonny.co.uk/home

Conclusion

Our hope is this book has offered you some ideas, insight and tools to support you in your work in the classroom with children who have SEMH needs. As we finish this book, we are about to start the new school year of 2024/2025. We will be working with the COVID-19 babies who are entering Reception classes, and in August 2024, an article was printed in the *Guardian* with alarmist suggestions that we are reaching a year where we will see some of the worst behaviour in classes (*Guardian*, 2024). We don't find articles like that very helpful! However, we are aware that the educator's job in the classroom is hard and we do know that more children are struggling and that has an impact on their learning.

We know that for some adults the idea of working with a child who becomes dysregulated and has high SEMH needs can be a frightening and anxiety-provoking prospect, we hope that this book has offered you a few tools to equip and support you, we believe that having some knowledge and insight and being fore-armed with a few simple tools can help you feel more prepared.

We have both worked in this area of education for over 10 years, however, we are still learning and adapting and adjusting our practice; in many ways, that is a fun side to our jobs, being able to adapt and change ensures the job never becomes boring.

We wish you well in your time in the classroom and we hope that some of these ideas will make a difference for you and the children in your care.

Thank you for reading this book and thank you for all the work you do with children, we believe working with children is one of the best jobs in the world.

Reference

Guardian (2024) 'Bubble' of post-pandemic bad behaviour among pupils predicted to peak. 25 August. Available at: https://www.theguardian.com/education/article/2024/aug/25/bubble-of-post-pandemic-bad-behaviour-among-pupils-predicted-to-peak?CMP=Share_iOSApp_Other

Index

Note: For picture citations, page numbers appear in *italics*.

ABCF tool 9–10
ADD *see* attention deficit disorder (ADD)
ADHD *see* attention deficit hyperactive disorder (ADHD)
adoption 5
adult care 38
adults, seeking out 33
affection 107
agitation 4, 33
alcohol abuse 5, 8
'all about me' bag 70
allen key 130, *134*
Amazon 94
animals 66; *see also* pets
Anna Freud charity 6
anxiety 2, 19, 22–3, 69, 103, 129, 151; toilet area 49–50
Apple Music 106
aroma dough 54
aromatherapy 47
art therapy 77
assembly 63, 68
attachment disorder 2
attention deficit disorder (ADD) 2
attention deficit hyperactive disorder (ADHD) 2, 57, 139
attention-seeking 20
autism 54

baby talk 4

bad reports 37
BBC (British Broadcasting Corporation) 6
beads 124, 128; threading 55; water 55–6
Benham, Fifi 40
bereavement 8, 75–7; puddle jumping 77; resources 78
bilateral brain exercises 137–48
biting 20
Black history month 43
blankets 42, 45–6
body language 9
body percussion 138
Bomber, Louise 54, 62
book corners *see* reading: corners
Bradbury, Julia 103
breakfast 64, 100–1
breaktimes 33
breathing 29, 121–4; activities 32, 56–7; balls 46; bee 123, *133*; blowing out candles 46; box 124; bubble 46; exercises 133; finger 46, 123, *133*; fist 137–8; home-made fidget toys 46; hot chocolate 123, *133*; jellyfish craft 122–3; petal 123, *133*; pipe cleaner stick 122; tools 46
Brown, Brene 11, 13, 22, 107, 109, 111
bubble wrap 128

155

INDEX

bubbles 51, 127; bubble mixture recipe 118
buddying 64
bug finding kit 50
bunny hops 32
burnout 107
butterfly hugs 137

caffeine 113
calling out 20, 33, 35–6
calm box ideas 127–8
calm kit 53, 69
Calm website 106
calming activities 31, 37; bottles 46, 125, 128; images 47; strategies 23, 25–6
Camhs (child and adolescent mental health services) 8
canopies *see* tents
carers 8, 15, 105, 137; foster 15; young 5
carpet spots 43–5, 56
certain subjects 35–6; struggling children 35; support for children 35–6
chair press-ups 138
chalk 50, 58, 87
'checking in' 36
chew toys 22
chews 55
child illness 5
Christmas 71
'chunking' work 36
class disruption 20
class instructions 20
class visitors 66–7
clay 83, 86, 89, 128; additional suggestions 89; basics 89
climbing activities 31
cloakrooms 48
cloud dough recipe 119
cognitive behavioural therapy (CBT) 8
Colilles, Sharon 43
colouring-in 31, 65; additional suggestions 88; basics 87; sheets 87–8

communication books 37
community culture 42–3
compassion *see* self-compassion
concentration problems 4
COVID-19 pandemic 2; behaviour, effect on 151; creativity and 80; mental health, impact on 6
crab walking 32
crafts 86, 89, 94, 122
crawling 32
creative writing 86, 92; additional suggestions 92; basics 92
creativity 80–96; benefits of 80; classroom examples 94–5; classroom practices 86–95; COVID-19 pandemic 80; help for children 82; methods 83–5; resources for adults 95; resources for children 95–6; right *vs* wrong way 82–3; wellbeing and 80–1
crocheting 85, 92–3, 113; additional suggestions 93; basics 92–3
crying 4, 12, 30, 36, 107
Csikszentmihalyi, Mihaly 81
cultural identity 15, 42–3
curling up body 4
cushions 42, 46, 56

'dance of attunement' 62
dancing 86; to music 31
deep pressure activities 56
defective-type skills 3
deficit model 2
Delahooke, Mona 4
den-making material 51
depression 2, 103
designing/sculpture 88; additional suggestions 88; basics 88
difference model 2
dining areas 48–9
discovery bottles 125–6, 128
disruption 35
distress 20
domestic violence 5, 8
drawing 31, 76; additional suggestions 87; basics 87; materials 83–4, 86–7

INDEX

drug abuse 5, 8
drumming 138; fingers 35–6
dysregulation 4, 10, 151; class regulation 19–22; individual children 28, 32, 35, 38; sensory needs 56; transitions 75

ear defenders 48–9
early years education 9–11, 41
eating disorders 2
educators 15
EHCP (educational health care plan) 5
Elsa (tool) 77
emergency accommodation 74
emotion(s) 11–13, 19, 28–9; framework 128; literacy 11–13; regulation of 82; stones/cards 128; words 109; see also regulation zones
end of the day 36–8; struggling children 36–7; support for children 37–8
environment 40–52; see also physical environment
ethnic identity 42–3
exercise 102–4, 107; cost and 103; individual preferences 104; mental health and 103; resources 114; time, lack of 103
eye contact 62

facial expressions 12, 20
facial images 46
fake snow recipe 119
families: bereavement 5; blended 5; break-up 5; mental health 5; new siblings 5; physical health difficulties 5; situational changes 74–6
Fearnley-Whittingstall, Hugh 100
feathers 128
feelings 'check-in' station 42
Feldman Barrett, Lisa 12–13
fidget toys 46, 56, 124–7; DIY 124–5
fidgeting 20, 22, 33, 55, 62
financial stress 5
fine motor skills: activities for 31, 149–50

fingers: mouthing 20–2; tapping 20
fish tanks 48
flow: concept of 81
flowers see plants and flowers
foetal alcohol spectrum disorder 5
food 99–101; breakfast 30–1; budget recipes 101; gut health 100; healthy eating 29; poverty 31, 101; recipe books 100; resources 114; ultra-processed 100–1
foster placement 76
fragrances 54–5; see also lavender
freeze response 37
friendship: good behaviours and 142–8; struggling to make 3
funding: challenges 2; mental health 7

games: cards 24; one-to-one time 38; 'Simons says' 24–5; 'Thumbs up, heads down' 25
Geddes, Linda 102
gender 15
glue therapy 58–9
Go noodle exercises 25
Goldsworthy, Andy 91
good behaviours 142–8
GPs (General Practitioners) 98, 103, 106
gratitude practice 29, 111
green spaces 108; see also time in nature
Grimmer, Tamsin 3, 8
Guardian newspaper 102, 105, 152
gym balls 31

hair brushing 31
Hampshire Child and Adolescent Mental Health Service 15
hands: massages 31, 46, 128; movements 20; washing 34
health conditions 100–2; close family members 5; see also mental health
hiding 3, 30, 33, 37
hopscotch 31
hot spots 23–4, 26
HRT (hormone replacement therapy) 105

157

INDEX

Hughes, Daniel 62
humming 35–6, 55
hunger 4, 12, 23
hurting others 4, 20, 34, 140

'I wonder' phrase 13
ice play 120–1
Imagination Tree website 118
imaginative play 51
individual child regulation 28–39
'investment pays dividends' 25–6

Japan: *shinrin yoku* (forest bathing) 108
jewellery making 93; additional suggestions 93; basics 93
jigsaws 31, 55, 64
Jordan, Sarah 66
jumping: trampolines 31

keyrings 124–5
kinetic sand 128
K'nex construction toys 84
knitting 92–3; additional suggestions 93; basics 92–3

lacing 31
Laevers, Ferre 11
languages 43
Latham, Katherine 105
laughing 107; inappropriate 4
lavender 54–5, 106, 118, 120; squish 127
leaving the classroom 35; at the end of the day 65
Lego 31, 37, 84, 128
legs and feet 138
Leicestershire City Council website 11
'let's squeeze orange juice' activity 57, 132, 137
Leuven scale 11

lighting 47–8
lining up 24
London Arts and Health 81
looking out of the window 62
loud and busy bodies 30, 37

loved ones: connectedness with 29
lunchtimes 33; dining area 48–9

Malaguzzi, Loris 41
massage: hand 31, 46, 128; peer 25; tools 55, 128
meditation: faith-based 29
Meek, Laura 66
memory function 103
menopause 105
mental health: attachment, resources on 78; children and young people 6–11; close family members 5; designated lead 7; exercise and 103; Government Green Paper (2017) 7; identifying needs 8–9; mental health support team (MHST) 7–8; observations 9–11
Mental Health Foundation 81, 112
mindfulness 25, 29, 111; resources 115
mirrors 47
Monroe, Jack 101
mood zones 40
morning arrival 64–5
mosaic making 93–4; additional suggestions 94; basics 94
movement breaks 22, 31, 55, 56, 139
moving: class 68–70; country 5; house 5, 73–4
multi-headed screwdriver 130, *133*
Murphy, Kerry 40
music: dancing to 31; making 86; for sleep 106; therapy 77

Nagoski, Amelia 107
Nagoski, Emily 107
National Centre for Creative Health 82
National Institute for Health and Care Excellence (NICE) 7
natural resources 42
nature art 51; additional suggestions 91; basics 91; pictures 91; *see also* time in nature
Neff, Kristin 109
neurodiversity 5, 43
new children arriving in class 70–1

158

new school 72–3
NF Schools website 91
NHS (National Health Service) 7, 102
'now and next' boards 34, 63, 149

observation sessions 20
obstacle courses 50
OT Toolbox website 46
outdoor area 50–1

painting 31, 51, 58, 87
pairing up 36
pandemic see COVID-19 pandemic
parents 15
PE (physical education) 69; changing for 33, 62
peers: interaction with 25, 33; massage 25; support 21
pets 70–1
PGCE (postgraduate certificate of education) 54
Philips, Joanna 66
phonics 32–3
photographs 66, 69–70, 73; of children 42; of staff 42
physical environment: children's own station/separate space 45; importance of 43–5; sense of space 44–5; space to move 43–4
picking skin 3
picture timetables 65–6
Pinterest 117, 125, 148
pipe cleaners 128
plants and flowers 42, 84–5; growing 51
play therapy 77
playdough 31, 54, 65, 127; gym 25; recipe 118
playtime 24
post-traumatic stress disorder (PTSD) 5
press-ups 31
printing 90–1; basics 90–1; found objects 90; natural objects 91; stamps 90
problem-solving 134
psychological safety 7

pulling: climbing bars 31; eyelids/body parts 20–1, 55; hair 3
pushing: body parts 21; tyres 31

quietness: body cues 62; calming activities 31; classrooms 34, 64, 140; corners 31, 55; fidget toys 46; quiet time 113

reading: corners 31, 42; silent 35; staff wellbeing 113
Reception class 69, 110
refusal to join in 4, 35
Reggio Emilia classrooms 41–2
regulation toolbox: rationale for 130; visuals 129
regulation zones 42, 45–7; ideas 46–7; resources 128; retreat 47; third teacher 41–2; toilet area 49–50; welcoming space 42
relationship-building 38–9
Relax kids 25
repeated movements 20
resistance bands 22, 128
resources 117–49; for regulation 127–8
retreat 47
rice stress balls 126
Richter, Max 106
rocking: chair 33, 62
roly-poly 32
routine: predictability of 63
Rowland, Mark 112
rubbing body parts 20–1
ruining work 35
rule books 130; importance of 135; rule-following 135
running: activities 31, 56; away 3, 37

sadness 4, 30
safeguarding children 75
scaredness 4
school parties 68
school trips 67
science experiments 67
sculpture see designing/sculpture
seating positions 43–4

159

INDEX

seed bags 128
selective mutism 4
self-choice mode 10
self-compassion 109–10
self-harm 2, 3, 55
SEND (special educational needs and disability) 54; Code of Practice 2
SENDCo (special educational needs coordinator) 7, 9, 32, 37, 70–1
senior leadership team (SLT) 7, 59
sensory activities 117; ideas 118–21
sensory aids 56
sensory circuits 24, 31–3
sensory needs 53–60
sensory overload 68
sensory processing disorders 54
sensory rice 54–6, 65; recipe 120
sewing 92–3; additional suggestions 93; basics 92–3
shared interests 39
shouting out 3
Siegel, Dan 13
silence 110; resources 115
silly voices 4
singing 35, 86
sitting position 56; problems sitting still 4
sketchbooks 83–4
skittles 51
sleep 103–6; alcohol, avoiding 106; bedtime routine 106; caffeine, avoiding 106; good sleep hygiene 106; issues with 106; lack of 14; natural light 105; nicotine, avoiding 106; patterns 105; recommendations for 105–6; requirement for 105; resources 115
Sleep Foundation 104–5
slime 54, 128
slinky toys 128
'small world' play 51
Smith, Julie 111
snacks 37
social, emotional and mental health (SEMH): concerns about 11;
contribution to needs 4–6; definition of 2–3; needs, symptoms of 3–4, 43–4, 151; outdoor areas, value of 50; statistics 5–6; struggles with 8–9
social stories 75, 78, 140
soft material 47, 127
sorting activities 31
Spector, Tim 100
spirit level 130
Spotify 106
squats 32
squishies 46, 127
staff wellbeing *see* wellbeing
star jumps 32
start of the day 24, 30–3; struggling children 30; support for children 30–3
starting points: prolonging 35
stillness 110; resources 115
storytelling 86
straight thinking 136
stress 73, 103, 105–7, 129; balls *see* stress balls; resources 115
stress balls 46, 127; rice 126; water bead 126–7
Structural Learning website 11
substance misuse 2; *see also* alcohol abuse; drug abuse
swimming 102–3; cold water 53, 104, 109, 111, 113; pool 53, 113
swinging 20–1, 31

tangles 46
tapping 21, 25, 55
teachers: change of 71; job-share 65–6
TED talks 81, 109
tensing and relaxing exercises 22, 56–7, 130, 132
Tension Tapping Technique (TTT) 25, 139
tents 42, 47
thread 128
threading 31
Thrive tool 6, 77
throwing objects 4, 33

INDEX

tidy-up time 34
time in nature 107–9; bringing the outside in 108; growing food or plants 108; outside exercise 108–9; resources 115; spending 108
tiredness 4
toilet area 49–50; anxiety 49–50; crowdedness of 50; smell of 49; transitions 33–4
toolbox *see* regulation toolbox
toys: construction 55, 84; regulation 42; *see also* chew toys; fidget toys; Lego; slinky toys
transitions 61–79; daily points 23; forewarning of 34, 63; key 33–4; major 72–7; medium 66–71; micro 33–4, 61–2; necessity of 63; playtimes 23–4; recognition of 62; support for 34, 62–6
trauma 5–6, 58, 139; informed approaches 7, 54
treasure hunts: sensory rice 31
treasure trails 51
trusted relationships 38–9
TTS 43
Twinkl 147

uncluttered spaces 42
uniqueness of children 15
unwellness 37

van Tulleken, Chris 100–1
violence 71, 112; triggers for 21
visual instructions 36

visual regulation reminders 46
visual timetables 34, 42, 45, 63, 147
vulnerability 22–3

water bead stress ball 126–7
water play 51, 121
welcome signs 43
welcoming space 42
wellbeing 26; acts of kindness 112; checking in with colleagues 112; creativity and 90–1; definitions of 97; emotional 106–9; physical 99–102; self-love and 98; spiritual 110–11; staff 22, 29, 97–116; supporting colleagues 112; toolkit 113
Welly name pegs 48
whole class regulation 19–27
'who's the strongest?' exercise 138
window of tolerance 13–15, 30
withdrawnness 3
wobble boards 22
word searches 31
work in-trays 36
workstations/desk areas 35–6, 44–5, 63

yawning 62
yoga 46, 108–9, 111; cards 128; resources 115
Yoshifumi, Miyazaki 108
YouTube 14–15; videos 151

zones of regulation *see* regulation zones

For Product Safety Concerns and Information please contact our EU
representative GPSR@taylorandfrancis.com
Taylor & Francis Verlag GmbH, Kaufingerstraße 24, 80331 München, Germany

www.ingramcontent.com/pod-product-compliance
Lightning Source LLC
Chambersburg PA
CBHW050527170426
43201CB00013B/2113